FINDING YOUR WAY

Navigating a World Changed by Pandemic and AI

John J. Polemis, CPC

You Are Who You Create, LLC
Cold Spring, NY

You Are Who You Create., LLC

YouAreWhoYouCreate.com

First Edition

ISBN-13: 979-8-9882805-0-7

This book is dedicated to my team, whose support and hard work in helping others cope with the challenges during the COVID-19 pandemic, even while struggling with the same challenges, have been truly heroic.
I am grateful to have such a supportive and dedicated team.

Anthony M.
Elias R.
Joann F.
John L.
Kerrie F.
Max S.
Patrick L.
Tony A.
Yeimy R.

Prefer a Hand's-on Workbook?

For those who prefer a more hands-on approach, I designed a companion workbook that provides various engaging, thought-provoking worksheets, tips, and journal prompts one can use to work through the various chapters of this book. It can also be used on its own as a general workbook for personal growth and self-discovery.

You do not need the workbook to benefit from reading this book, but it is a valuable supplement for those wanting to dig deeper into the material presented here in a more structured way.

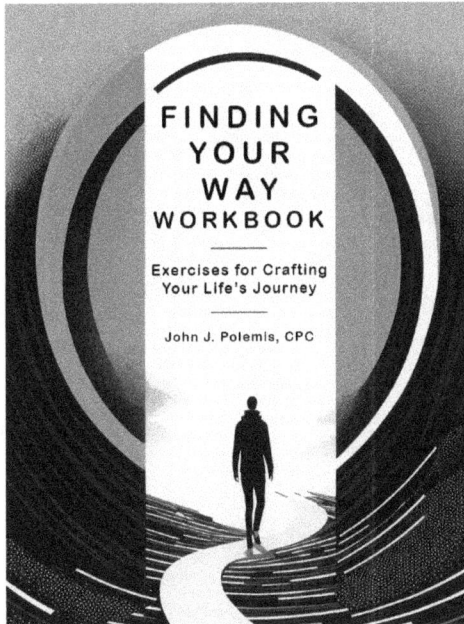

FINDING YOUR WAY WORKBOOK

Exercises for Crafting Your Life's Journey

John J. Polemis, CPC

Title: Finding Your Way Workbook

ISBN-13: 979-8-9882805-1-4

CONTENTS

CONTENTS

Throwing a Lifeline...

The COVID-19 pandemic has had a significant impact on the state of mental health worldwide, exacerbating existing mental health conditions and contributing to new ones. The uncertainty, fear, isolation, and economic challenges associated with the pandemic have created a perfect storm for mental health struggles, affecting people of all ages, backgrounds, and walks of life.

Individuals have faced - and continue to face - numerous stressors, such as job loss, financial insecurity, grief over the loss of loved ones, and the disruption of daily routines. It's been rough on all of us, and some have weathered it better than others by no fault of their own.

If you are having difficulty coping with these challenges and uncertainty or struggling with depression, anxiety, feelings of isolation, or other mental health concerns leaving you feeling overwhelmed, you need not struggle alone. Professional mental health support, such as support groups, therapy, or counseling, can provide individuals with the tools and strategies to manage their symptoms and improve their overall well-being.

There are many free hotlines, community services, non-profit organizations, and support groups for those who need them. Some employers offer EAPs, which provide free, confidential counseling and support for employees dealing with personal or work-related issues, including mental health concerns. While I am more cautious with religious options due to a possible lack of training on mental health issues, that, too, is an option for those who are more comfortable taking that route.

Telehealth services have become increasingly accessible and popular during the pandemic, providing a safe and convenient way for individuals to connect with mental health professionals remotely. This increased accessibility has allowed many who may have otherwise faced barriers to care, such as transportation or geographical limitations, to receive the support they need.

If you are having thoughts of harming yourself, I am raising the red flag for you now - it's time to ask for help, regardless of how hopeless things seem.

Early intervention is crucial in addressing mental health concerns, as it can help prevent the worsening of symptoms and the development of more severe mental health conditions. Unfortunately, a byproduct of struggling with mental health concerns is a sense of hopelessness and negativity that can make it difficult to imagine being able to move past one's current feelings and difficulties. This is a *symptom*, not a fact.

I wish you well on your journey, and while I hope you will find value in this book, please remember that books, online courses/videos, and motivational talks can only go so far and are never a substitute for professional help when it is needed.

Introduction

As I brainstormed a title for this book, I was reminded of the many post-apocalyptic movies where a sole survivor struggles in the hardships of the vast wastelands. Well, on the bright side, the pandemic was not THAT bad, eh? Regardless, the world has changed, and for those not ready, this new post-pandemic world can feel like a wasteland full of hardship and danger. For others, this same world is full of new opportunities and flexibility, breaking them out of the old suffocating ways of the world before the great shakeup of the pandemic. The reality is, BOTH worlds exist today, and the choice in which world we live in is purely upon us. It may not feel like much of a choice at the moment, and that, my friends, is what inspired me to write this book.

Ironically, most of this book's topics are nothing new to the pandemic. What has happened is the pandemic has shaken things up enough in our lives to force us out of our old comfort zones. By doing so, we have already taken the first critical (and perhaps most difficult) step on the journey of self-discovery and personal transformation. It is only natural to want to return to the comfort of the way things were, and in cases where that is still possible, we would ultimately lose this precious opportunity for growth.

As a certified professional coach specializing in personal transformation, I'm a bit of a fan of shakeups. Transformation comes from struggle, and while we may find being pushed out of our comfort zones uncomfortable and not appreciating the challenges we were thrust into without preparation, the seeds of personal transformation and evolution have been sewn. We did not have much choice in how we got here, so this book is here to help you make sense of it all and equip you with the tools, strategies, and insights you need to navigate this new era confidently. We'll dive into a wide range of topics, from embracing the new normal and cultivating a growth mindset to developing new skills and adapting to the AI-driven workplace. The goal is not to tell you what to do but rather to help you develop the skills, self-discovery, and vision needed to move you closer to becoming the person you want to be and living the life you want.

The fact that you are reading this book is an excellent sign you have already chosen to move forward from this place of difficulty, so let's take this journey together.

How this book is organized

This book is broken down into four parts:

In **Part 1**, we will address the primary motivation most will have behind purchasing this book: coping with change and uncertainty, especially due to the lingering effects of the COVID-19 pandemic and the rapid emergence of AI. However, there are undoubtedly other global events in the news that may also contribute to our unease these days! The intended takeaways from this section of the book are discovering our purpose in life and developing a resilient mindset to help us move forward with direction while coping with change and uncertainty.

In **Part 2**, we will build on the skills from Part 1 by nurturing a growth mindset to enhance our resilience and make the most of our challenges. We will start taking action to recover from any adverse effects of the pandemic that might have hindered your progress and seek to find balance in this "new normal."

In **Part 3**, we will concentrate on our well-being, ensuring a holistic approach that encompasses our physical, mental, and emotional health. We want to ensure we support ourselves and find others to support us. Self-care strengthens our resilience to adversity and change, empowering us to move forward with intention and self-compassion.

In the final section, **Part 4**, we will integrate everything we've learned about ourselves and the skills we've developed while working through parts 1, 2, and 3 and apply this knowledge to our career and professional life. The end game is to find meaning, direction, and resilience in our professional lives.

Each chapter will build upon the next, so I encourage you to take time as you work through the book. Consider starting a journal to document your journey through this book. This will make it easier to track progress and return later to revise your work further.

Before jumping onto part one, be kind to yourself here. If I may let my New Yorker out for a moment, we have all gone through some rough shit! The last few years have been challenging. This is where you can begin to put things back in order, even better than before. Give yourself time to learn and heal. Be patient with yourself and know that with every effort you make, you are one step closer to the improvement you desire and one step further from the stresses that brought you here.

You got this!

Part 1

Moving Forward

CHAPTER ONE

Embracing the New Normal

The COVID-19 pandemic has profoundly shaped our lives - from how we work and socialize to how we shop and travel. The phrase "new normal" has become a ubiquitous metaphor for these profound changes. While some aspects of our lives may eventually return to pre-pandemic patterns, others remain permanently altered. I can't imagine ever returning to a two-hour commute twice a day like I used to do before the pandemic - it seems impossible that this could ever be considered "normal!" The "old normal" wasn't perfect - it just existed and made it difficult to see beyond its familiar confines. What other parts of that same "old normal" are we still holding onto out of ignorance of greater possibilities?

Now, with artificial intelligence (AI) beginning to make an impact, we're entering a "new normal" in ways we are only just beginning to comprehend. I am reminded of when social media first took off. Though we had some concerns that it could be misused, we could never have imagined just how deeply embedded (if not habituated) it would become into daily life and how easily misused. The same can be said of the internet, personal computers, and smartphones - all of which have become staples in modern living. All these developments have had profound effects, bringing risks and uncertainties to how we live and work. Careers were affected, and work-life balance was severely disrupted, yet new opportunities emerged as well. After living through all these transformations for so long, I find the advent of easily accessible powerful AI to be even more significant; its potential risks to those unable or unwilling to adapt are truly frightening.

As you read through this book, I urge you to approach the new normal with curiosity and openness. Consider how these changes have or could impact your own life and consider potential growth opportunities that they present. Change and uncertainty can be scary but exciting opportunities for self-discovery and innovation. Ultimately, change is an inevitable part of life; by accepting it and finding meaning, you'll unlock new possibilities that enrich your journey. The more resilient and adaptable you become, the higher your chances are of success and contentment along the way!

If you are feeling stressed or overwhelmed with the new normal, take a deep breath, try your best to relax, and remember: you are not alone here. One positive side of these changes is that we're all trying our best to come to terms with them in our own way - even me! I wrote this book intending to help all of us on this challenging journey together - including myself!

A Strategic Approach

In response to the challenges of the pandemic, new ways of working, socializing, and living have emerged – and continue to emerge – and we must be open to embracing these changes or risk unnecessary stress and hardship. It requires flexibility, adaptability, and a willingness to learn new skills. This starts by acknowledging that the world has indeed changed and that some of these changes are here to stay, whether we like them or not. Allow yourself time to grieve the loss of the "old" normal, but be ready to accept and adapt to the "new" normal as you move forward to build the life you want for yourself.

Drawing from my experience as a transformation coach, I propose tackling this effort in areas of focus, each of which aligns with the four parts of this book as outlined below. Ultimately all of these areas are interconnected, but this logical breakdown allows us to organize our efforts and better visualize the key components of what is at play here.

1. Taking ownership and responsibility

The first step on this journey is to understand just how much we shape our lives, consciously or not, through how we choose to view and respond to our experiences. How we perceive challenges, changes, and uncertainty plays a role in creating the opportunities (or drama) we find in our lives. The key thing is that we can learn to adjust how we perceive these challenges. In the rest of this first part of the book, we will explore how we can choose to adapt and respond to change and difficulties and, in the process, build resiliency that will help carry us through these and future life challenges. The rest of this first part of the book will help you lay the groundwork needed to support you on this journey.

Whether we thrive or struggle to survive in this new normal relies heavily on how we choose to approach it. While we may have certain default dispositions to which we have become habituated, it is important to understand that our mindset is changeable. We can learn better ways of perceiving our experiences and the world around us, and we can choose how we want to respond to them in ways that promote our personal growth, well-being, and overall success in life. It can take time to develop these skills and train the brain to default to more beneficial mindsets, so give yourself some space to work through that process.

2. Prioritizing personal growth

Developing a growth mindset (the belief that intelligence, talent, and abilities can be acquired through effort, learning, and persistence) contributes to how we adapt and thrive by cultivating a problem-solving approach to challenges. Focusing on the opportunities for growth and learning that have emerged from the pandemic, rather than dwelling on the negatives, empowers and motivates us to move forward, tackling challenges as they come. This is very much a skill that can be learned with practice and persistence.

3. Prioritizing and managing one's well-being

Adjusting to the new normal also involves caring for one's mental and emotional well-being and building support structures with self-care practices. This might mean seeking support from friends, family, or mental health professionals and developing coping strategies to manage stress, anxiety, and other emotional challenges. It's important to be patient with yourself and others during this time of transition, as everyone's journey will be unique. As we will explore, there is much more to self-care than meditation and vacation days.

4. Adapting to new work-life structures and adjusting one's career path

The pandemic has significantly changed how we work, with remote work and flexible working arrangements becoming more common. With all these changes, it's a good time to reevaluate career goals and identify areas for upskilling.

Tackling these four areas might feel overwhelming and challenging initially, but with patience and a proactive approach, you'll be able to adapt and thrive in this ever-evolving landscape. Ultimately this is not about a quick fix but instead about developing the skills and setting the goals needed to support you on your journey. The rest of this chapter will help lay the foundation needed to get the most out of this book and help you navigate the change and uncertainty in your life and find your way in this new world.

CHAPTER TWO

Foundational Skills

Foundational or "keystone" skills are skills that can have a significant impact on various aspects of one's personal and professional life. These skills often serve as building blocks for other skills, making them essential for success and personal growth. They can also be referred to as core skills, soft skills, or transferable skills.

In this chapter, we'll touch on specific foundational skills which will support you as you work through this book. Throughout the book, you'll be introduced to skills, many of which would be considered foundational. But for now, let's keep to the basics and lay out a strong foundation upon which to build. The skills to follow later will draw upon that foundation.

Some of these skills may seem like common sense or even trivial to you, while for others, they can seem unrealistically achievable. As skills, regardless of natural talent or current level, there is always room for further development. These are not things one learns and checks off as "done." These are skills one will continue to develop over time as they are applied in various ways in one's life. If they feel difficult for you, that is fine! Give yourself the time you need to practice them. They will get easier, but only if you keep working with them!

I recall when I had joined a krav maga school that taught martial arts by packaging it as a fitness program. The workouts at the beginning of class were military-grade and brutal! At the end of my first class, I limped out of the gym, thinking I would never fit in. One of my fellow new classmates posted a cute meme on the social media page that said, "The difficult workouts of today are the warmups of tomorrow." I scoffed but held firm to my commitment to at least give it the six weeks the initial challenge called for. Besides, I had put money up to keep me accountable that I would only get back if I stayed the full six weeks! Somewhere in the middle of that challenge, I came to a sudden realization... that brutal workout at the start of the class was, in fact, the warmup! It was only once my body had time to adjust and strengthen that I was able to push through these "warmups" and be ready for the martial arts practice portion of the class. Moreover, by the end of that six-week challenge, I would notice new members half my age struggling to keep up as I had been and how a few commented to me after class how it felt like they would never be able to keep up. My point here? If a lazy middle-aged geek like me can get to that point of fitness, then there is a world of possibilities out there for all of us willing to put in the time and effort. Challenge your comfort zones, but be kind to yourself too.

As you read through the rest of this chapter, consider these questions:

1. Where else can these skills be applied in your life?
2. What aspects come naturally to you?
3. What aspects feel challenging or impossible?
4. What are some ways you could improve or build upon these skills?
5. What goals can you set to support you as you develop these skills?

Nurturing a Positive Mindset

When facing a challenging circumstance, it can be easy to forget that we have the power to frame it in ways that either assist or hinder us. Recognizing and making that choice may come more naturally to some than others; however, any skill can be developed through practice and repetition.

Our perception of an experience shapes how it impacts us emotionally and mentally. How we choose to interpret an event or scenario determines how we process, respond, and ultimately remember it.

Some ways in which our perception can shape the impact of an experience are:

1. Cognitive Appraisal: Our perception of an experience begins with our cognitive appraisal of the situation. This involves evaluating potential threats, challenges, or opportunities an event presents. If we perceive it as a challenge or opportunity, we are more likely to have a positive emotional response and see it as an opportunity for growth; on the contrary, if we perceive it as a threat, we are more likely to feel negative emotions like fear or anxiety.

2. Emotional Response: How we perceive an experience shapes our emotional reaction. When we view a situation positively or as an opportunity for growth, we tend to feel more upbeat, confident, and motivated; conversely, a negative perception may lead to stress, anxiety, or sadness.

3. Coping Strategies: Our perception of an experience shapes the coping strategies we employ to manage it. A positive perception may motivate us to act, problem-solve, or seek support; conversely, a negative perception could result in avoidance, denial, or rumination.

4. Resilience: Choosing to perceive an experience positively can foster resilience, or the capacity to adapt and recover from adversity. By focusing on our strengths, learning from them, and maintaining a positive outlook, we can build resilience and better prepare for future difficulties.

5. Memory and Future Expectations: Our perception of an experience shapes how we remember it and anticipate similar ones in the future. If we perceive an event positively, we are more likely to remember it positively and approach similar situations with optimism; conversely, a negative perception can lead to negative memories and expectations, potentially shaping our behavior restrictively going forward.

Here are some examples to illustrate how one's perception of an experience can shape them:

1. Job Loss:

- Negative Perception: If a person views losing their job as a failure, they may experience feelings of shame, guilt, and hopelessness. This mindset could squelch motivation to search for another job, and prolonged unemployment could negatively impact one's self-esteem and well-being.

- Positive Perception: If someone views job loss as an opportunity to explore new career paths and acquire new skills, they may feel more optimistic, motivated, and enthusiastic about the future. A positive mindset can encourage proactive job searching and hasten recovery from setbacks.

2. Public Speaking:

- Negative Perception: If someone feels anxious about public speaking and perceives it as a terrifying experience, they may feel overwhelmed and unable to deliver an effective speech. This negative perception could also reinforce their fear, making them more likely to avoid future public speaking opportunities in the future.
- Positive Perception: Conversely, if they view public speaking as an opportunity to share their expertise, connect with an audience, and hone communication skills, they will likely feel more confident and inspired. This positive outlook could result in better performance and increased enthusiasm for future public speaking assignments.

3. Relationship Breakup:

- Negative Perception: If someone views a breakup as an irreparable loss and reflection of their unworthiness, they may experience intense feelings of sadness, rejection, and loneliness. This negative outlook could hinder their capacity for healing from the breakup, potentially impacting future relationships and overall well-being.
- Positive Perception: Viewing the breakup as an opportunity to grow as an individual can help them recover more quickly from it and create stronger relationships in the future. A positive outlook may enable them to navigate challenging times better and build healthier bonds in the future.

4. Receiving Criticism:

- Negative Perception: If someone takes criticism personally or as an indication that they lack competence, they may become defensive, frustrated, and demotivated. This negative mindset prevents them from learning from feedback and progressing personally or professionally.
- Positive Perception: Ultimately, if they see criticism as constructive criticism and an opportunity for growth and improvement, they are more likely to feel open-minded, receptive, and motivated to make changes. This mindset can contribute to their personal and professional development by encouraging a growth-oriented outlook.

These examples illustrate how our perception of an experience can significantly affect our emotional, mental, and physical well-being. By cultivating a more optimistic and growth-oriented mindset, we can better navigate life's obstacles while increasing resilience and well-being. Ultimately, it's up to each of us whether to survive or thrive in this new world.

Shifting Perceptions

To improve your perception of an experience, try these strategies:

1. Practice mindfulness: Becoming more in tune with your thoughts and emotions can help you identify and combat negative perceptions while developing greater self-awareness and emotional regulation.
2. Reframe the Situation: Seek a different perspective or search for the positive side of things. Reframing can help you recognize opportunities for growth, learning, or beneficial outcomes.
3. Cultivate gratitude: Recognizing and expressing appreciation for the positive aspects of your life can help shape your perspective, making it easier to find the good in even difficult circumstances.
4. Seek Support: Reaching out to friends, family, mentors, or a professional coach or counselor can give you an objective viewpoint and valuable insight into the experience, potentially altering your perception. It's often easier to see alternative perspectives through others' eyes rather than one's own.

5. Develop Self-Compassion: Accept that setbacks and challenges are part of life, and treat yourself with kindness and understanding. Self-compassion will help you keep a more balanced perspective on your experiences.

By choosing to view experiences more positively, you can reduce their impact on you and develop greater resilience and emotional well-being.

Cultivating Mindfulness and Presence

Mindfulness and presence are often used interchangeably, yet there are subtle distinctions between them.

Mindfulness is the practice of cultivating non-judgmental awareness of one's thoughts, emotions, bodily sensations, and environment in the present moment. It involves developing focused attention on an experience while accepting it without judgment or distraction. Mindfulness often includes techniques like meditation, deep breathing, or body scanning to help individuals increase self-awareness and emotional regulation.

Presence, on the other hand, is a state of being fully present and focused on what needs to be done at that moment. It requires paying full attention to whatever task or situation arises without allowing thoughts to drift back or forward in time. Presence naturally arises through practicing mindfulness but can also be fostered independently through an intentional focus on being in the present moment.

Many times, mindfulness and presence are seen as essential self-care practices (which they certainly are), but it also serves as a building block for various personal and professional abilities. Some of the skills that benefit from having mindfulness as an underpinning element include:

1. Emotional Intelligence: Mindfulness helps you become more conscious of your own and others' emotions, giving you insight into how best to manage and navigate social interactions.
2. Stress Management: Mindfulness techniques such as meditation and deep breathing can help reduce stress levels by encouraging relaxation and increasing self-awareness.

Additionally, these exercises enable us to identify triggers of our anxiety so that we can respond intentionally rather than reacting out of habit.

3. Focus and Concentration: Mindfulness can enhance your ability to stay focused and concentrate on tasks by eliminating distractions, improving mental clarity, as well as inducing a more present state of mind.

4. Active Listening: Mindfulness helps us remain fully present during conversations, leading to deeper comprehension and more efficient communication.

5. Conflict Resolution: By developing an empathic awareness of one's feelings and those of others, mindfulness can help you approach conflicts with empathy and lead to more constructive resolutions.

6. Decision-Making: Mindfulness provides insight into your thoughts, emotions, and values so you can make more informed and balanced decisions.

7. Self-regulation: Mindfulness can help you recognize and manage your impulses, thoughts, and emotions more effectively, leading to improved self-control and emotional stability.

8. Adaptability: Mindfulness helps you become more aware of your environment, equipping you to respond to changes with flexibility and resilience.

9. Creativity: Mindfulness encourages an open and curious mindset which promotes creative thinking and problem-solving abilities.

10. Self-Compassion: By cultivating nonjudgmental awareness of your thoughts and emotions, mindfulness can help you build greater self-compassion and acceptance of yourself.

As you can see, incorporating mindfulness into your daily life can enhance a variety of skills and contribute to both personal and professional growth. Cultivating mindfulness leads to an enhanced sense of well-being, resilience, and personal growth even during times of major life transitions.

(We'll talk more about how we can use mindfulness specifically when coping with change and uncertainty in the next chapter.)

* * *

How to Become More Mindful and Present

Gain the benefits of mindfulness by adding practices such as meditation, mindful breathing, or body scans into your daily routine. Start with just 5 minutes daily and gradually increase the time until it feels comfortable - up to 10-15 minutes.

Explore ways mindfulness can be integrated into your everyday life to enhance the experience. For instance, try not to do tasks around the house or walk somewhere on autopilot - something we do more than we realize - but rather be fully present and aware of all senses and thoughts as you do them.

By incorporating mindfulness techniques into your daily life, you can cultivate the skills and mindset needed to successfully navigate life's inevitable changes and uncertainties with greater ease and assurance. Journaling, which I will explore more in-depth in the following section, can significantly benefit your mindfulness practice. I highly recommend using a journal as you progress through this book!

Here are a few common mindfulness practices you can try out. There are plenty of free resources online with more exercises. If you have the companion workbook for this book, I have included plenty of exercises and a worksheet to help log your practice and monitor results.

Meditation

There are countless styles of meditation that can lead one down some interesting paths. Here's a step-by-step guide for an easy breath awareness meditation suitable for beginners or practitioners of any level, especially beneficial when cultivating mindfulness. This practice helps you focus on your breath, develop present-moment awareness, and train your mind to be less distracted.

1. Select an area with few distractions where you can sit or lie down comfortably for the duration of your meditation.
2. Sit with your back straight, either on a cushion, chair, or the floor. You may also lie down if sitting is too uncomfortable. Place your hands on your lap or sides for added support.
3. Gently close your eyes to reduce external distractions and focus on breathing. There is no need to force them closed if you find them cracking open a little.

4. Inhale slowly through your nose, filling your lungs. Then exhale slowly through either mouth or nose. Repeat this several times to center yourself and relax.

5. Let your breath return to its natural rhythm without trying to force it. Pay attention to the sensation of breath moving in and out of your nostrils or the rise and fall of your chest or abdomen as it moves.

6. Pay close attention to the sensation of each inhalation and exhalation. Take note of the length and depth of your breath and any pauses between breaths.

7. It is usual for the mind to wander during meditation. When you notice that your thoughts have wandered, gently acknowledge them and bring your focus back onto your breath.

8. While you meditate, strive to maintain an attitude of non-judgment and self-compassion. Accept any thoughts, emotions, or sensations that arise without criticism or frustration; be a passive observer.

9. Begin with a short session of 5-10 minutes and increase the duration as you become more adept at the practice.

10. When your timer goes off or you feel ready to conclude your meditation, slowly bring awareness back into the present moment. Open your eyes, wiggle your fingers and toes, and take a few deep, cleansing breaths before getting up.

Breathing Exercises

Breathing exercises are an excellent way to cultivate mindfulness, as they help focus your attention on the present moment and promote relaxation. Incorporating these breathing exercises into your daily routine can reduce stress and boost focus. Be patient with yourself as you practice; eventually, it will become easier to maintain a mindful state of being.

Here are a few breathing exercises I personally prefer to utilize. Listen to your body for the correct durations, and consult your doctor if any medical conditions restrict breath capacity or performance.

1. Diaphragmatic Breathing (Belly Breathing):

1. Sit or lie down in a comfortable position with your spine and

chest straight.
2. Place one hand on your chest and the other on your abdomen.
3. Take a slow, deep breath through your nose, allowing your abdomen to rise while keeping your chest still.
4. Exhale slowly through either your mouth or nose, letting your stomach drop back down.
5. Repeat for several minutes, focusing on the rise and fall of your abdomen.
6. As your mind wanders, gently bring your attention back to the sensation of breathing.

2. Box breathing (aka square breathing or four-fold breath):

1. Sit or lie down in a comfortable position.
2. Inhale slowly through your nose for a count of 4; hold that breath for four counts.
3. Exhale slowly through your mouth or nose for a count of 4.
4. Pause for a count of 4 before inhaling again.
5. Repeat this cycle for several minutes or until you feel more mindful and relaxed.
6. As your mind wanders, gently bring your attention back to the sensation of breathing or counting.

3. Alternate nostril breathing:

This exercise can seem complicated, but once you try it, you will see it is relatively straightforward. For the hand you will use to close the nostrils, fold your index and middle fingers into your palm, extending your thumb, ring finger, and pinky finger. This tends to be the most comfortable.

1. Sit down comfortably with your spine to be erect and your chest open.
2. Close your eyes and take a few deep breaths, inhaling and exhaling through your nose. Allow your breath to become slow and steady.
3. Use your right thumb to close your right nostril gently.
4. Slowly inhale through your left nostril, counting to four as you fill your lungs with air.
5. Use your right ring finger to gently close your left nostril while keeping the right nostril closed with your thumb. Hold

your breath for a count of four.

6. Release your thumb from your right nostril, keeping your left nostril closed with your ring finger. Slowly exhale through your right nostril, counting to four as you release the breath.

7. Keep the left nostril closed, and inhale through the right nostril, counting to four as you fill your lungs with air.

8. Use your thumb to close your right nostril again, keeping the left nostril closed with your ring finger. Hold your breath for a count of four.

9. Release your ring finger from your left nostril, keeping your right nostril closed with your thumb. Slowly exhale through your left nostril, counting to four as you release the breath.

10. Repeat the process for a few minutes or as long as you feel comfortable. Aim for at least 5-10 cycles to experience the full benefits of alternate nostril breathing.

11. After completing your practice, release your hand from your face and return to natural breathing through both nostrils. Take a moment to observe how you feel physically and mentally before opening your eyes and resuming your day.

Body Scan Exercise

A body scan exercise is a mindfulness technique that involves mentally scanning your entire body from head to toe, paying attention to any sensations, tension, or discomfort you may feel. This practice helps cultivate present-moment awareness, strengthen the mind-body connection, and promote relaxation. I've even found this exercise beneficial when struggling to fall asleep - just don't be surprised if you don't make it all the way through!

Here's a step-by-step guide on how to perform a body scan exercise to become more mindful:

1. Sit or stand with your feet flat on the ground and back straight, or lie down on a mat or bed with arms by your sides, palms facing up.

2. Gently close your eyes to reduce external distractions and help you focus on your body.

3. Start by taking slow, deep breaths through your nose and out through your mouth; this will help you relax and focus your mind's attention.

4. Begin by paying attention to the sensations throughout your entire body. Pay attention to points of contact between yourself and whatever surface you're sitting or lying on; feel its weight; any feelings of warmth, coolness, or tingling?

5. Start at the top of your head and move awareness down through it, visualizing a warm glow enveloping each part as you bring focus onto them. You can follow this sequence or choose another order that feels more natural to you:
   - Forehead, eyes, cheeks, jaw, mouth
   - Neck and shoulders
   - Arms, elbows, wrists, and hands
   - Chest and upper back
   - Abdomen and lower back
   - Hips pelvis buttocks Thighs knees calves and shins
   - Ankles, Feet, and Toes

6. As you scan each body part, note any sensations such as tension, warmth, coolness, tingling, or discomfort. Observe these feelings without judgment or attempt to change them; simply be present with each sensation as it arises.

7. If you are in moments of tension or discomfort, imagine directing your breath toward those areas. As you exhale, visualize releasing tension and relaxing muscles.

8. Once you have observed and breathed into a particular body part, gently shift your focus to the next area in your body scan sequence.

9. If your mind wanders during a body scan, gently bring it back to the part of the body you were focusing on. Be kind and patient with yourself throughout this practice.

10. Once you've scanned your entire body, take a moment to appreciate it. Then, slowly bring your focus back onto your breath by taking several deep, cleansing breaths.

11. Slowly open your eyes, wiggle your fingers and toes, touch your face, and take a deep breath as you reacquaint yourself with your environment.

Journaling

Journaling is an invaluable tool for personal development and productivity, offering numerous advantages, from emotional well-being to improved self-awareness to better organization skills. In this section, we'll examine the benefits and types of journaling and provide tips for getting started with this practice. I highly recommend using journaling while working through this book to better process and apply what you are learning.

What Are The Benefits of Journaling?

Journaling can have numerous advantages for personal development and productivity. Here are a few of the more notable ones:

1. Improved mental clarity: Journaling helps organize your mind, leading to improved decision-making and problem-solving abilities.
2. Emotional Processing: Writing down your thoughts and feelings provides a safe space to express and work through emotions, which can contribute to emotional well-being.
3. Enhance Self-Awareness: Journaling can give you valuable insights into your values, beliefs, patterns, and personal growth by reflecting on experiences.
4. Stress Reduction: Writing down your thoughts and emotions on paper can reduce stress and anxiety by providing a platform for self-expression.
5. Goal Setting and Tracking: Journaling can serve as a vehicle for setting, tracking, and reflecting on personal and professional objectives, helping you stay focused and motivated.
6. Boosting Creativity: Writing regularly unlocks your creative potential by stimulating fresh ideas and perspectives.
7. Healing & Personal Growth: Journaling can promote healing and personal growth by helping you process past experiences, learn from them, and move forward.
8. Enhancing Gratitude and Positivity: Recognizing and celebrating the positive aspects of life by journaling can improve your overall well-being and contentment.
9. Better communication skills: Journaling can improve your ability to express yourself verbally and in writing by clarifying

your thoughts and emotions.

10. Historical Record: Those who have been journalling for a long time have the benefit of being able to look back over their history to see how they have evolved and also discover patterns that may not be noticed otherwise.

Types of Journaling

There are various types and techniques of journaling available, depending on your needs and interests. Some common options are listed below; pick one that resonates with your requirements or combine elements from different types to create a practice that supports personal growth and self-expression best for you.

1. Personal Journal/Diary: A personal journal is an outlet for recording thoughts, emotions, experiences, and reflections on daily life. It can assist with self-awareness, emotional processing, and personal growth.

2. Gratitude Journal: Maintaining a gratitude journal can help you focus on the positive aspects of life and encourage gratitude. Regularly recording what you are thankful for can foster an optimistic attitude and enhance overall well-being.

3. Dream Journal: Dream journals are used to record and interpret dreams, which can increase self-awareness and comprehension of your unconscious mind and uncover hidden insights and patterns.

4. Art Journal: An art journal is a creative outlet that combines visual artwork with written reflections, providing space for self-expression and exploration. It can include drawings, paintings, collages, and mixed-media artwork.

5. Bullet Journal: A bullet journal is an organizational system that combines a planner, a to-do list, and a diary. It utilizes symbols called "bullets" to prioritize tasks, events, and notes in an organized and concise fashion.

6. Goal-Setting Journal: Goal setting is the practice of setting, tracking, and achieving personal and professional objectives. It can aid with motivation, accountability, and personal development.

7. Guided Journal: Guided journals provide structured prompts and exercises to help you reflect on specific topics or areas of

personal growth. You can find these journals under various themes like self-discovery, creativity, and mindfulness - making them invaluable tools for breaking out of boxed-in thinking or when one struggles to come up with topics to write about.

8. Career Journal: Maintain a career journal to track your professional objectives, successes, and experiences. This can help you reflect on your path in the workplace, identify strengths and areas for improvement, as well as plan for the future of your profession.

9. Idea Journal: An idea journal is a place to store creative thoughts, brainstorm during sessions, and be inspired. This can help you hone and develop your creative abilities and keep track of inventive ideas.

10. Habit Tracker: Habit trackers are tools used to monitor and assess the consistency of specific habits or daily routines over time. You can develop new behaviors, break unhealthy patterns, and reach personal objectives more efficiently. By visually representing your progress on a chart, habit trackers provide motivation, increase self-awareness, and hold you accountable for your choices.

Some prefer keeping separate journals for each function they require, while others opt for one that serves all needs. There's no one way to go about this - I currently prefer keeping both a general journal and a productivity journal. My general journal serves mainly as a place for my daily reflections but also includes gratitude journaling, interesting dreams, hiking adventures, and even the occasional doodle. My productivity journal serves to track projects and goals and draft ideas. When taking on bigger projects or learning a new skill, I prefer dedicating an entirely separate journal just for that. This is what works for me, but you may have your own approach.

Getting Started

When starting the practice, don't stress over frequency or type of journaling. Try a few styles of journalling and gradually adapt the practice to fit your individual style and preference. Have fun experimenting! The key is not letting all these options get in the way of actually beginning the practice. By exploring various types of journaling and following the tips provided below, you can develop a journaling routine explicitly tailored for you.

1. Determine the Media: Determine whether you prefer journaling in a physical notebook or an electronic platform. Each option has advantages and drawbacks, so pick which option best meets your requirements and preferences. If unsure, choose whatever works best for you - you can always switch later once you understand what works best or use both types depending on what is most convenient at the time. Ultimately the best media is the one you find most accessible and likely to be used.

2. Establish a Regular Time For Journaling: Make time to journal regularly, whether daily, weekly, or whenever you feel the urge. Consistency is the key to reaping many of the rewards of journaling. However, while making this a regular habit is ideal, avoid stressing over frequency. Some of the other tips below will help with keeping consistency.

3. Create a Comfortable Environment: Create a peaceful and relaxing atmosphere to journal in, free from distractions. Doing this will help you focus and make the most out of your sessions. That said, remember this is just an ideal situation to encourage the journaling practice. It is more important to take advantage of any opportunity to journal instead of waiting for the most perfect time that never comes.

4. Use Prompts: Journaling prompts can be an excellent starting point if you're stuck for what to write about. They can be questions, statements, or topics that encourage self-reflection and exploration; many can be found online. If you own the companion workbook for this book, I also included many of them there. Prompts are also a great way to break out of our usual thinking patterns and consider things we may not otherwise have considered.

5. Be Honest With Yourself: Remember that your journal is a private space where you can be completely honest with yourself. Express your genuine thoughts and feelings without fear of judgment or criticism.

6. Don't stress over grammar or structure: Journaling should be seen as a vehicle for self-expression, not perfection. Focus on

getting your thoughts and emotions down on paper without worrying about grammar, spelling, or sentence structure.

7. Start Slowly: If you're new to journaling, begin with short sessions of 5-10 minutes and gradually increase the duration as you become more adept at the practice.

Don't stress over what journal to use if you are just beginning. Any notepad can do the job; if need be, grab some loose sheets of paper from your printer. Typing is fine if you prefer it; using your word processor or favorite note-taking app should do the job. The important part is to start writing and focus on developing the habit and skill of consistent journaling. Keep things simple for now. Once you become more comfortable with journaling, it will become easier to identify your preferences and adjust accordingly. Chances are your preferences will evolve over time as well. Years ago, I used a digital journal, but lately, I'm back to basics by using an elegant hand-bound paper journal and well-crafted fountain pen - it helps me slow down and appreciate the experience of writing more deeply.

Overcoming Common Journaling Challenges

Journaling can be rewarding, but it's not without challenges. Here are some common journaling difficulties and suggestions on how to overcome them:

1. Lack of Motivation or Inspiration: It's common to experience a lack of motivation when beginning or maintaining a journaling practice. To combat this obstacle, try using prompts or themes as inspiration. Make time each day for journaling and make it part of your routine; additionally, experiment with different styles or techniques for greater engagement and fresh ideas. Trick: when stumped about what to write, journal about that! You may find yourself writing more than you expected as you ponder why your mind went blank.

2. Perfectionism: Many people struggle with perfectionism when journaling, which can prevent them from expressing themselves authentically. To combat this, remind yourself that your journal is a safe space for exploration and self-expression - not to create an impressive piece of writing. Allow yourself to write without judgment or expectation and embrace the journey of self-discovery. Let go of the need for perfect entries

- remember, journaling aims to express yourself authentically, not produce flawless work.

3. Time Constrained: Finding time to journal regularly can be a real struggle with a hectic schedule. To conquer this obstacle, commit to journaling for some time each day - even if it's only 5-10 minutes! Try using timers, writing in bullet points, or using voice-to-text apps as shortcuts in the process. Consider times when you are a captive audience, such as in a waiting room or on a train.

4. Privacy Concerns: Some people worry about their journal's privacy and the possibility of others reading their thoughts. To address this concern, consider using a digital diary with password protection or storing your physical journal securely. Alternatively, develop a personal code or shorthand to keep writing private.

5. Writer's Block: Feeling stuck when trying to maintain a journaling practice can be discouraging. Try free writing without self-censorship, using prompts, or setting a timer for short writing bursts to combat it. Changing your environment or journaling at different times of the day might also spark creativity.

6. Consistency: Establishing a consistent journaling practice can be overwhelming. To make it work for you, set specific goals like writing daily for one month or filling up certain pages. Create an accountability loop by journaling at the same time each day and tracking your progress to stay motivated.

7. Judging Your Thoughts and Emotions: It is essential to approach journaling with an open mind and a non-judgmental attitude. If you judge yourself as you write, remember that your journal is a place for exploration and self-discovery. Embrace self-compassion and try not to judge your emotions without judgment.

8. Fear of Judgment from Others: Remember that your journal is a private and judgment-free zone. You need not share your journal or even the fact that you have a journaling practice if you do not choose to. You have the option to share your thoughts with others, but only when you feel ready.

9. Getting Started: For some people, facing a blank page can be

intimidating. To overcome this obstacle, write a brief prompt, quote, or question at the top of the page to provide direction and make starting easier. At worst, write about not knowing what to write about!

Remember, the key to conquering journaling difficulties lies in persistence and patience. Experiment with different techniques and approaches until you find what works best for you, and always approach your practice with self-compassion and eager curiosity.

CHAPTER THREE
Coping with Change and Uncertainty

Coping with change and uncertainty is a fundamental life skill that profoundly affects one's personal, professional, and psychological growth and well-being. Navigating these inevitable difficult circumstances helps individuals build resilience, maintain mental health, and develop adaptability in an ever-changing world. Accepting change and uncertainty offers opportunities for self-discovery, personal growth, and problem-solving skills. Furthermore, it strengthens relationships by encouraging empathy, effective communication, and conflict resolution. Ultimately, adapting to these changes contributes to increased self-assurance, life satisfaction, and overall well-being, allowing individuals to lead more satisfying, meaningful lives.

This chapter will examine the typical stages of change, the significance of acknowledging uncertainty, and how to develop adaptive coping strategies to survive in our ever-evolving world.

Understanding the Stages of Change

Change often unfolds in stages, and understanding these stages can help us better manage our emotions and responses. Common stages of change include denial, resistance, exploration, and acceptance. By recognizing the stage you're in, you can develop more effective coping strategies and work toward embracing change with a positive outlook.

It is only natural to feel the way you do; these stages are a natural part of the coping process. The question is, how will you choose to respond?

Denial Stage

In the denial stage, individuals may refuse to acknowledge the reality of change or underestimate its impact on their lives. They might hold onto their previous routines and beliefs, hoping things will return to how they were.

To move forward, it's essential to confront the reality of change and recognize that some aspects of life may never return to how they were. Remember that denial is a normal part of the change process, serving as a defense mechanism to protect oneself from overwhelming emotions. Chances are you will realize you are in the stage through the feedback of others since denial is easier to recognize in others than in oneself. If you find yourself vehemently protesting in denial about something, it is a good indicator that some self-reflection may be needed. Keep an open mind and learn more about the situation you find yourself denying, cultivating curiosity. Give yourself the needed time to process at this stage.

Resistance Stage

During the resistance stage, individuals may feel angry, fearful, or overwhelmed by the prospect of change. They might actively oppose or resist adapting, even when they recognize its necessity or benefit. It's crucial to understand that these feelings are natural and that it's okay to experience discomfort during the process of change. Seeking support from friends, family, or professionals can help individuals work through their resistance and build resilience.

This stage offers a wonderful opportunity for self-exploration. Identify the underlying reasons for your resistance, such as fear of the unknown, loss of control, or perceived negative consequences. How does this relate to your core needs and values? Resistance can often indicate a conflict with them. Consider how your needs and values can be addressed through the change. Approach with a problem-solving mindset to explore options that would make the change in question work to your benefit.

Exploration Stage

In the exploration stage, individuals become more open to the idea of change and seek information and resources to help them adapt. This stage involves curiosity, learning, and experimentation as people explore new ways of thinking and behaving. It's important to maintain a growth mindset and be willing to take risks and learn from mistakes during this stage.

Research and gather information about the change, available options, and potential outcomes. This will help you make informed decisions and better understand what is involved in the change process. What goals can you set which would help you better manage the change? For example, during the pandemic, an unfortunate change many experienced was having their jobs furloughed or terminated at a time when finding work would be especially difficult. This forced people to research what programs were being made to address this crisis, how to better budget expenses, and explore alternate sources of income to get by the best they could until new job opportunities became available. Some tried self-employment, offering various professional services, and learning the entrepreneurial process along the way. Others reskilled into new professions they may not otherwise have considered out of fear of taking a professional risk.

Acceptance Stage

At the acceptance stage, individuals fully acknowledge and embrace the reality of change. They have worked through their initial resistance and are now actively adapting to the new circumstances. Acceptance involves integrating new habits, routines, and perspectives into one's life, leading to a more balanced and fulfilling existence in the face of change.

Take time to consider the lessons and insights gained throughout the change process and acknowledge the challenges you've overcome and the growth that has occurred as a result. Celebrate your successes. If, during that journey, you identified areas that could use more attention, such as things you feel you could have handled better, set some goals to move forward with your personal development.

Recognizing and understanding these common stages of change can help individuals better acknowledge and accept the changing and uncertain life experiences they will inevitably encounter. By being aware of one's emotional responses and thought patterns during each stage, one can develop targeted strategies and seek appropriate support to facilitate smoother adaptation. Embracing change is an ongoing process, and maintaining a flexible and resilient mindset will enable individuals to thrive in a constantly evolving world.

Developing Adaptive Coping Strategies

Adaptive coping strategies can help us manage the stress and uncertainty associated with change. One's ability to cope with changes will affect one's mental health and outlook on life. Those struggling to cope with a change in one's life might be left with feelings of negativity about the outcome, such as bitterness or regret. Such people may need more time and some additional support to get back on track. Meanwhile, those who are more resilient in the face of change may find they can bounce back and adapt to that change more readily.

Regardless, there are some steps that one can take to make the adjustment easier. Identify healthy ways to cope with change while avoiding maladaptive coping strategies, such as substance abuse or denial, which can exacerbate stress and hinder personal growth. Be open to trying new things and learning from your experiences, and remember to practice self-compassion, as change is an inevitable part of life for all of us.

Focus on what you can control.

Take a moment to consider the things that you can control when you are worried about change. Although you cannot stop a storm, you can prepare yourself for it. You cannot control what someone else does, but you can choose how you respond. You'll be more productive if you focus your energy on the things that you can control. Concentrating on what you cannot control disempowers you and only serves to fuel your worry and stress.

Concentrating on controllable aspects reduces anxiety and stress, increases self-efficacy, and encourages proactive problem-solving. Moreover, maintaining a positive outlook and fostering a growth mindset helps us view change as an opportunity for learning and self-improvement. By adopting this approach, we can more effectively navigate change and lead a more fulfilling and adaptable life. We will explore this more in the chapters on building resilience and a growth mindset.

Practice Self-Compassion and Self-Care

Life will throw enough difficulty our way, so we need not add to that stress ourselves. Dealing with change can be difficult and messy. There may not always be an ideal solution, just less terrible ones. Building a resilient mindset will help us better bounce back from setbacks and challenges, but it is important to be forgiving and remember that we are doing the best we can with where we currently are. Learn from your mistakes, identify areas you can improve, and give yourself space to learn and heal. When you are struggling, show yourself the same level of support you would for a friend in the same situation. Find the support you need to help you move forward, which includes self-support as well as from one's community and professionals.

Additionally, one's resilience is dependent upon one's well-being. Be sure to attend to one's basic needs: proper sleep, nutrition, and physical and emotional health. Consider your well-being the foundation for any coping strategy, so it must be well fortified. When things are at their worst, it is all the more vital that you prioritize your well-being so that you have the right mindset and energy level available to you in such times of need.

Remember, everyone's journey is unique, so explore different approaches and find the best strategies for you. Stay patient and persistent, and be kind to yourself.

Finding Positive Meaning in Change

In team meetings, I have always found it interesting how differently various members of the team will view a given change. Some will be excited, some indifferent, and others fear what it means for their future or take personal offense. Ultimately the meaning we assign to something will reflect our beliefs and values. Changes we perceive as aligned with our beliefs and values will carry positive associations. Changes that conflict with our beliefs and values will be seen as threats or trigger a strong emotional response.

Finding meaning in change starts by reflecting on one's core values and how they may be connected to the changes you're going through. Acknowledging the potential opportunities for growth and learning these changes offer can lead to a deep sense of contentment and fulfillment. Expressing gratitude for lessons learned while engaging in activities aligned with your values and purpose further equips you to better accept and embrace inevitable changes. When the changes bring stress, explore what is at stake here. What is the perceived threat? This may hint at a value conflict or negative belief.

Consider the impact of a company adopting automation and artificial intelligence (AI) to streamline processes and boost efficiency. This change may be perceived differently depending on one's core values and beliefs.

An individual who appreciates innovation, progress, and technology may view this shift as a positive development that will propel their company forward and keep it competitive in the market. They may see the potential for increased productivity, reduced human error, and improved overall performance. Furthermore, this individual may believe embracing new technologies is essential for the business's long-term success and might look forward to learning and working with cutting-edge AI tools and systems.

Conversely, someone who values job security, human connection, and tradition may view the same change event differently. They could be concerned about potential job loss due to automation, fearing machines could replace them or their colleagues. They might also worry that AI implementation will create a depersonalized work environment which reduces opportunities for collaboration and human connection. These beliefs could cause them to resist change as they feel the company is sacrificing employees' well-being in pursuit of technological progress.

These two opposing perceptions illustrate how one's core values and beliefs can shape their interpretation of a change event. The same change could be seen as an opportunity for growth and innovation or a threat to job security and human connections, depending on an individual's values and beliefs.

Finding *positive* meaning in change can give us a renewed sense of purpose and optimism, especially in uncertain times. Change presents numerous opportunities for growth, learning, and personal development - it acts as a catalyst for self-discovery while encouraging resilience and adaptability even during difficult times. We can tackle change with greater optimism by approaching it with curiosity and an eagerness to learn and adapt.

In the above example, the individual who sees the company's use of AI as worrying has valid concerns. However, fear and stress bring no value, so that person could, for example, explore how they personally could make the best of that change. For instance, if the fear is about job security, taking this as an opportunity to learn how to leverage AI tools in the workplace would add value to that individual and possibly lead to a new role. If the concern is a depersonalized work environment, perhaps this offers an opportunity to explore new ways to ensure collaboration, maybe even while leveraging the new technology, opening the door to innovation.

Change can be an opportunity for growth and transformation - approaching it with curiosity, openness, and a willingness to learn and adapt is a skill anyone can adopt, but as with any skill, it may require some practice to make it available when facing a triggering change.

In the next chapter, we delve into how to identify one's core needs and values to make this process easier. In part 2, we explore how to cultivate a growth mindset, which is essentially the keystone skill at play when finding positive meaning in change.

Understanding One's Emotions

Emotions play an integral role in our well-being, decision-making, and relationships. To better comprehend your feelings, practice naming them without judgment. Ponder the triggers behind your emotional experiences and consider how they shape your thoughts and decisions. You can develop healthier coping strategies and improve your emotional intelligence by cultivating emotional awareness.

Understanding your emotions is fundamental to finding purpose and direction in life. This practice will help manage your emotional well-being, allow you to manage change effectively, and foster personal growth as you adjust to new circumstances and challenges. Once we identify and process our feelings, we can respond productively rather than blindly. Furthermore, understanding where our emotions may have caused us harm could reveal itself in subtle ways: perhaps giving up on projects when feeling overwhelmed; or letting anger over a situation impact professional and personal relationships without realizing it.

Emotional intelligence (EI) is the capacity to recognize, comprehend, and regulate one's emotions and those of others. Emotional intelligence facilitates effective communication and empathy with others and encourages personal development on all levels - more so than one's IQ, which measures cognitive ability! EI has even been shown to be more important for personal and professional success than IQ alone!

Here are some tips to help you better comprehend and manage your emotions, drawing upon mindfulness and self-reflection.

1. Establish Emotional Awareness: Begin by paying attention to your feelings as they arise. Notice any physical sensations, thoughts running through your mind, and any external triggers that might be contributing to them. What are your emotions telling you?

2. Label Your Emotions: Name your feelings to help identify and accept them. Doing this can give you an increased sense of control and clarity. Common emotions include happiness, sadness, anger, fear, surprise, and disgust; however, many nuanced emotions exist to explore.

3. Accept Your Emotions Without Judgment: Emotions are a normal part of life, so allow yourself to feel them without judgment. By acknowledging and accepting your feelings, you can better process and manage them more effectively.

4. Reflect on the source of Your Emotions: Consider possible causes of your feelings. Are they connected to an event, relationship, or something deeper in you? By understanding where these emotions come from and developing healthier coping mechanisms, you can address underlying causes and develop more beneficial coping methods.

5. Recognize Patterns and Triggers: As you reflect on your emotions, look for patterns or triggers that might have

contributed to them. For instance, certain situations, people, or environments may frequently elicit certain emotions in you.

6. Examine Your Thoughts: Your thoughts and beliefs can significantly affect how you feel emotionally. Take note of any recurring thoughts, assumptions, or beliefs that might contribute to these experiences; are they accurate or distorted in some way?

7. Practice Self-Compassion: Show yourself kindness and empathy as you confront your emotions. Remember that everyone experiences a range of feelings in their own way, so treating yourself with understanding and compassion is essential.

8. Develop Healthy Coping Strategies: Once you've gained insight into your emotions, develop effective methods for dealing with and managing them. This could involve engaging in self-care activities, seeking support from others, practicing mindfulness techniques, or challenging unhelpful thoughts and beliefs.

9. Consider Professional Support: Consulting a mental health professional, such as a therapist or counselor, could be beneficial if you're having difficulty understanding or managing your emotions. They can offer guidance and comfort as you work through these feelings.

CHAPTER FOUR

Finding Purpose and Direction

In my coaching practice, I can't count the number of times I hear clients say something to the effect of "I feel like I have no direction in life," so they find themselves just getting by, feeling stuck and frustrated. Not a great feeling... I know; I have been there myself! Perhaps it's a right of passage we all have to go through at some point. What I do know is sometimes life circumstances will veer us off course from our inner purpose and direction, and even when we cannot clearly articulate that purpose, we know something is wrong, and we are not where we want to be. It is then that we know it is time to roll up our sleeves and clarify where we want to go in life so that we can take actionable steps to bring our lives back on course.

Feeling one lacks purpose and direction is not a sign of failure - it is a call to action!

Finding Purpose

Finding purpose and direction in life involves discovering what truly matters to us and pursuing our passions, values, and strengths to create a meaningful life. By doing so, it can provide us with motivation, satisfaction, and well-being, guiding our choices and actions to stay on the desired path even during storms that might threaten to throw us off course.

Here are a few tips to help you discover your purpose and

direction in life. We will cover them more fully throughout this book. Note how the fundamental skills we already discussed play a role here and how these various tips interact with one another. As I said before, "building a solid foundation" applies here; these guidelines serve as scaffolding that will support us as we grow into the person we desire to become and create the life we envision for ourselves.

1. Reflect on Your Needs and Values: Identify the values most important to you, such as honesty, love, or creativity. Your values can serve as a compass that guides decisions about how and what to pursue in life.

2. Explore Your Passions and Interests: List activities, hobbies, or subjects that genuinely excite and motivate you. These will be the areas where you feel most engaged and alive.

3. Identify Your Strengths and Skills: Recognize your natural abilities, acquired skills, and areas of expertise. Knowing these things about yourself can help you determine how to contribute meaningfully to the world.

4. Set Inspiring Goals: Define goals that reflect your interests, strengths, and values. These should be challenging yet achievable to add to your sense of purpose and fulfillment.

5. Cultivate a growth mindset: Embrace the idea that you can always learn, develop, and improve. A growth mindset will enable you to conquer challenges, adjust to change, and remain dedicated to your purpose.

6. Connect With Others: Connect with like-minded individuals who share your interests, values, and objectives. These contacts can offer encouragement, motivation, and a sense of belonging.

7. Give back: Get involved in activities that benefit others, such as volunteering, mentoring, or participating in community projects. Helping others can give you a sense of purpose and fulfillment.

8. Reflect and Reevaluate: Regularly assess your goals, values, and passions to ensure they align with your purpose. Be willing to modify as you learn and develop.

The Importance of Reflection and Introspection

I can't help but be reminded of the famous maxim "Know Thyself." These were the words inscribed in the entrance area of the Temple of Apollo in Delphi in ancient Greece. It was Plato who transmitted this phrase via his dialogues, where he suggested the importance of looking inwards before making any decisions or taking action. So it makes sense, in a chapter about finding direction, that we start with the skills needed to know ourselves better. After all, how can we know where we want to go if we do not first know who we are?

Reflection and introspection are essential for self-awareness, personal growth, and emotional well-being. By taking the time to understand our inner experiences, we can gain valuable insights into our emotions, behaviors, values, and motivations, allowing us to make more informed decisions, resolve conflicts, and cope with stress more effectively.

Below are some ways reflection and introspection tie in as keystone skills to other areas we are covering in this book:

1. Self-awareness: Reflection and introspection help us develop self-awareness, which is crucial for understanding our thoughts, emotions, and behaviors. By being more self-aware, we can make more informed decisions, regulate our emotions, and better understand our motivations and values.

2. Learning from experiences: Reflecting on our experiences, both positive and negative, allows us to learn from them and identify patterns in our behavior. This learning process can help us make better choices, adapt to new situations, and ultimately grow as individuals.

3. Coping with change: The post-pandemic world is marked by significant change and uncertainty. Reflection and introspection can help us better understand and cope with these changes by identifying our strengths, weaknesses, and areas for improvement.

4. Clarifying values and priorities: Reflecting on our values and priorities can help us align our actions with our beliefs and goals. This alignment is crucial for leading a more meaningful and fulfilling life.

5. Emotional processing: The process of introspection allows us to acknowledge and process our emotions, which is essential

for maintaining emotional well-being. Understanding and managing our emotions can enhance our resilience and better navigate the challenges of a post-pandemic world.

6. Strengthening relationships: Reflection and introspection can also help us gain insight into our relationships with others. By understanding our interpersonal dynamics, communication patterns, and emotional needs, we can work on improving our connections and fostering healthier, more supportive relationships.

7. Problem-solving and decision-making: Reflecting on our experiences and thoughts can provide new perspectives and ideas for solving problems and making decisions. This cognitive process can enhance our creativity, critical thinking, and decision-making skills, ultimately leading to more effective solutions.

8. Personal growth and development: Engaging in reflection and introspection fosters personal growth and development by allowing us to identify our strengths, weaknesses, and areas for improvement. We can become more adaptive, resilient, and successful in a post-pandemic world by continually working on ourselves.

9. Setting and achieving goals: Reflection and introspection can help us set realistic and achievable goals based on our values, priorities, and experiences. By regularly assessing our progress and making adjustments as needed, we can stay on track and work towards desired outcomes.

10. Cultivating gratitude and positivity: Reflecting on our experiences can help us develop gratitude and positivity as we acknowledge the good things in our lives and learn from our challenges. This mindset shift can enhance our overall well-being and resilience in a post-pandemic world.

Creating a Self-Reflective Routine

Developing a regular practice of reflection and introspection can help you harness their benefits more effectively. Consistency is key here, as it is with improving any skill. Set aside time each day or week for quiet contemplation, journaling, or meditation, and use this time to explore your thoughts, feelings, and experiences. Be patient with yourself and approach your practice with curiosity and openness.

Here are some tips to help you create an effective self-reflective routine:

1. Set aside dedicated time: Choose a specific time of day or week for your self-reflection practice. It could be in the morning, evening, or during a designated break. Consistency is key, so find a time that works best for you and commit to it.

2. Choose a comfortable space: Find a quiet, comfortable space where you can focus on your thoughts and emotions without distractions. This could be a cozy corner in your home, a quiet park, or even a coffee shop with a relaxing atmosphere.

3. Use a journal or digital tool: Writing down your thoughts can help you process them more effectively. You can use a physical journal, a digital app, or any other tool that works best for you. The act of writing can also help you track your progress and growth over time.

4. Develop prompts or questions: To guide your self-reflection, create a list of questions or prompts that help you explore your thoughts, feelings, and experiences. Some examples include:

   - What are my successes and challenges from today/this week?
   - How did I handle difficult situations, and what can I learn from them?
   - What am I grateful for?
   - How well am I aligning my actions with my values and goals?
   - What areas of my life require more attention or improvement?

5. Use mindfulness techniques: Incorporate mindfulness exercises, such as deep breathing, meditation, or body scanning, to help you focus your attention on the present moment and become more attuned to your thoughts and emotions.

6. Reflect on your relationships: Consider the quality of your relationships with others. Reflect on your communication patterns, emotional needs, and any areas where you could improve your connections.

7. Set actionable goals: Based on your reflections, set specific, measurable, achievable, relevant, and time-bound (SMART) goals for personal growth and improvement. Break down larger goals into smaller steps and track your progress.

8. Review and adjust: Periodically review your self-reflective routine and make adjustments as needed. You might find that specific prompts or questions are more helpful than others or that a different time of day works better for you.

9. Be patient and compassionate: Reflection and introspection can sometimes bring up difficult emotions or realizations. Be patient with yourself and practice self-compassion. Remember that personal growth is a lifelong journey, and being kind to yourself is essential during the process.

10. Share your reflections with others (optional): If you feel comfortable, consider sharing your thoughts and insights with a trusted friend, family member, or therapist. They may offer additional perspectives, support, or guidance.

While these tips will support your efforts, keep them from hindering you. For example, long before the pandemic, when I was focusing on developing self-care practices, I kept skipping my morning meditation practice because I was having trouble doing it at the time and place most ideal for it. Eventually, I realized it was more important to be consistent than do it perfectly. I started to meditate on the train to work, and while it had more distractions, it ultimately helped me to learn to work better through such distractions. It also helped me learn to be more flexible and loosen up on my perfectionist ways, which often hindered my movement.

Identifying One's Needs and Values

Unconsciously or not, our needs and values shape our decisions, affect how motivated and successful we feel, and ultimately determine whether goals are achieved. When these needs and values are fulfilled and respected, they can serve as a life compass that keeps us focused on what matters most for a happier, fulfilling life. Thus, goals aligning with core needs and values have much higher odds of being reached.

A **need** is an essential need for human survival, such as food, water, shelter, and safety. These needs can range from physiological to psychological in origin and are generally universal across all humans, although we may prioritize them very differently. Some may be willing to sacrifice privacy for convenience, while others would find such an idea unacceptable. During the lockdowns of the pandemic, I managed just fine with reduced social contact since my need for personal development allowed me to pursue my hobbies and passions more fully; at the same time, many friends and colleagues who struggled with isolation reached out to me and others for support.

Conversely, values are deeply held beliefs or principles that guide a person's behavior, choices, and attitudes. Values can differ across cultures, societies, and individuals due to personal experiences, upbringing, and cultural background. Values shape priorities, goals, and decision-making processes, while needs guide essential aspects of human functioning and survival. Values themselves are neither good nor bad; how they are reflected in our lives determines their significance. I value independence and problem-solving highly, which helped me adjust to the changes brought on by the pandemic but could also make asking for assistance difficult. Therefore, when facing difficulties, I must be mindful that these values may prevent me from seeking help when necessary. Developing self-awareness is key to making the most out of our values.

Unfortunately, we may not always be able to articulate our needs and values clearly, and they may sometimes conflict. When one feels they lack purpose or direction in life, starting by identifying needs and values can be a powerful step in finding clarity.

Needs vs. Strategies

As I worked toward my certification in coaching, one of the biggest obstacles many of my classmates and I faced when learning about needs was distinguishing them from strategies. Coaching requires digging deeper, so while someone may say, "I need more money" or "I need a new job," they are really saying what they believe they need to satisfy an underlying need or value that may not even be identified yet. Such assumptions often limit possibilities at best and, at worse, don't honor underlying needs at all, leading one down a frustratingly unfulfilling path.

For instance, I may think I need a new job, but on reflection, I realize that my dissatisfaction was due to not utilizing my creative potential. If I have not identified and sought to address my need for a creative outlet, I may simply trade one unfulfilling job for another. Perhaps happiness and success could be achieved at my current workplace by exploring how to leverage my creativity better.

Even if a strategy is beneficial, focusing solely on it can limit other opportunities to support one's needs and open doors to new possibilities. Fixating preconceived notions may cause us to think small; for instance, the famous "I need more money" strategy. Yes, more money can be helpful, but those who believe it will bring happiness and solve all problems should look no further than the experiences of many lottery winners to understand that money often receives far more credit for bringing joy than it truly deserves. Sure, having more money can be nice (when used responsibly), but should our happiness solely depend upon its acquisition? Are there truly no other ways to be content? If you are in debt, money can help, but there are other steps one can take at the moment, such as creating and adhering to a budget, devising a financial repayment plan, speaking with one's creditors to reduce penalties and interest, or exploring ways to generate extra income through selling unnecessary items or working a side gig. In the end, paying off one's debt AND learning how to manage it is needed - money is just one way that makes that happen. Keep in mind, too, that money alone here is a bandaid. If I have not learned how to manage my finances better, I will end up back in debt soon enough. The struggle to get out of debt is more likely to be transformative and thus have a lasting positive impact on one's life.

Identifying Strategies

Strategies are tailored to particular circumstances, people, and situations rather than being universal, like a "real" need that describes a shared human experience. A helpful way of identifying a strategy is through the PLATO technique: whenever we include a **P**erson, **L**ocation, **A**ction, **T**ime, or **O**bject in our expression of what we want, it becomes a strategy rather than simply an unmet need.

Identifying Needs

Here are some ways to recognize your core needs:
1. Self-assessment: Take time for self-reflection and introspection

to analyze your thoughts, emotions, and behaviors. Consider when you feel most satisfied, contented, or fulfilled, and identify what causes these feelings.

2. Prioritize: List your basic needs, such as safety, food, shelter, love, and belonging. Rank them in order of importance to better understand which are your top priorities. You can also find long lists of needs online, which you can rate to see which are more important than others.

3. Journaling: Keep a daily journal to record your thoughts, emotions, and experiences. Pay attention to patterns or recurring themes that indicate underlying needs or desires.

4. Analyze Past Experiences: Reflect on instances where you felt unfulfilled or frustrated. Consider which needs weren't met during those instances.

5. Identify Stress Triggers: Recognize situations that cause stress or anxiety. Stress often arises when needs are unmet, so understanding these stresses can help uncover those core needs.

6. Seek Feedback: Ask friends, family, or colleagues for their perspectives on your needs and behavior. Others may notice patterns you are unaware of, providing invaluable insights into the core needs.

7. Utilize Self-Assessment Tools: Complete self-assessment questionnaires or exercises like Maslow's Hierarchy of Needs to understand your core needs better.

8. Consult a Professional: Speak with a therapist, counselor, or coach who can guide you through identifying and meeting your core personal needs.

Remember, identifying your core needs may take some time, and your requirements may evolve as you grow and mature. Regular self-reflection and evaluation can ensure you stay in touch with these basic human requirements.

Determining Values

Values are the guiding beliefs, principles, or ideals which guide a person's behavior, decision-making, and lifestyle. They anchor moral judgments, shaping one's sense of right and wrong and setting priorities and objectives. Core values become deeply embedded in an individual's identity through upbringing, cultural background, personal experiences, and reflections.

Some common core values include honesty, integrity, compassion, respect, responsibility, family loyalty, equality, and personal growth. These concepts help individuals navigate personal and professional lives by providing a framework for making consistent and meaningful decisions.

Here are some ways to help you identify your core values:

1. Reflect on peak experiences: Think about moments when you felt most fulfilled, proud, or contented. Identify which values were present or reinforced during those times.

2. Consider Role Models: Draw inspiration from those you admire and respect, whether they be friends, family members, public figures, or historical figures. Consider what qualities and values these people exemplify that resonate with you.

3. Recognize Values in Action: Pay attention to your behavior and decision-making processes. When presented with difficult choices, reflect on which values guided your choices.

4. List Your Values: Create a list of values that resonate with you, such as honesty, compassion, loyalty, and ambition. Narrow down your list by ranking them in order of importance or significance to you.

5. Journaling: Keep a journal to record your thoughts, emotions, and experiences. Look for recurring themes that highlight values that are important to you.

6. Analyze Past Decisions: Reflect on past decisions, especially when you had to compromise or forgo something. Determine which values guided those choices and which ones you prioritized.

7. Utilize Self-Assessment Tools: Conduct value assessment exercises or questionnaires such as the Personal Values Card Sort or Rokeach Value Survey to uncover your core values.

8. Seek Feedback: Share your values with friends, family, or a mentor to gain their perspectives and provide you with helpful observations that can help clarify your core principles.

Similar to your core needs, identifying your core values is an ongoing endeavor that may change as you gain new experiences and perspectives. Regularly revisiting and reassessing these values helps ensure they align with personal development initiatives.

Identifying One's Passions

Identifying your passions is a necessary step toward living an enriching life. By acknowledging the activities and interests that excite and motivate you, you can make more informed decisions about personal and professional pursuits.

Here is a brief guide to help you uncover these interests:

1. Reflect on Your Interests: Start by listing the activities, hobbies, and subjects that have kept your attention throughout the years. Consider which ones bring you joy, satisfaction, or a sense of accomplishment.
2. Recall Your Peak Experiences: Think back on moments when you felt deeply engaged, fulfilled, or proud of what you accomplished. Analyze these events to uncover common themes or activities related to your interests.
3. Pay Attention to Your Energy Levels: Pay attention to how you feel when engaging in various activities. Those which energize you or make time seem like it passes quickly are usually linked to your interests.
4. Seek Feedback From Others: Reach out to friends, family members, or colleagues who know you well and ask them for their opinion on what drives you most. An outside perspective may reveal passions you hadn't noticed before. What can they not shut you up about?

Setting Clear and Meaningful Goals

So you have started using self-reflection to identify your needs, values, and passions to give you some purpose in life. But how do you find *direction*, as in, how do you live a life of purpose? In short: it doesn't tend to come naturally! Direction must be *actively* sought by setting clear and meaningful objectives which you can then work toward achieving.

Goal setting can be tricky, so I'll keep things simple and provide helpful strategies, advice, and examples to help get you on track with your life's journey. Setting clear goals is essential since the more precise one's objectives are, the easier they become to reach. As you read through this book, consider what goals you can set to apply what you've been learning as you go along.

Here are some tips that will aid your goal-setting efforts. There are also plenty of free goal-setting templates online. If you have the companion workbook for this book, I have included the template my team uses when setting their annual career goals and that I use myself when setting all my objectives.

Consider the 5 W's of Goal Setting

The 5 W's of goal setting provide a straightforward framework for creating clear and achievable objectives. They draw inspiration from journalism's 5 W's (Who, What, When, Where, and Why) when gathering information about a story. Here's how each W relates to goal setting:

1. What: Clearly define the goal you wish to reach. Be specific when discussing desired outcomes so your objective is well-defined and actionable.

2. Why: Consider the motivations and underlying reasons behind pursuing your goal. Understanding why it's essential for you can help keep you committed and focused during trying times. Reflect on how achieving the objective aligns with your values, interests, or long-term aspirations; ask yourself, "Why do I want to achieve this goal?" and "What will it bring into my life?"

3. Who: Identify those involved or affected by your goal. This could include yourself, family members, friends, colleagues, mentors, etc. Consider enlisting their support, motivation, or collaboration in achieving it.

4. When: Establish a realistic timeframe for achieving your goal. Set deadlines and milestones to stay on track and create urgency. Ensure the timeline is challenging enough to keep you motivated but achievable, given available resources and constraints.

5. Where: Decide the location or context in which your goal will be pursued. This could include physical spaces such as a workplace or gym or more abstract ones like a career,

relationship, or personal growth area. Knowing this helps create an effective plan and gather the necessary resources to reach success.

By considering the 5 W's of goal setting, you can craft an effective strategy for reaching your objectives. This approach guarantees you a clear understanding of why these objectives exist and the steps necessary to make them come true.

Make Your Goals SMART

SMART goals are a widely used framework for creating practical and achievable objectives. The acronym stands for **S**pecific, **M**easurable, **A**chievable, **R**elevant, and **T**ime-bound. Here's an overview of each component with examples and helpful hints:

Specific: Your goal should be precise and well-defined, addressing a particular outcome or objective. Vague goals make it difficult to measure progress and achieve them.

Example:

- Vague Goal: "I want to get fit."
- Specific Goal: "Run a 5K race in under 30 minutes."

Tip: Use the 5 W's (Who, What, When, Where and Why) discussed above to ensure your goal is precise and clearly expressed.

Measurable: Your objectives should be quantifiable or assessable, enabling you to track progress and determine when you've met them. Doing this makes tracking progress much easier, plus it keeps you motivated!

Example:

- Non-measurable Objective: "I want to improve my public speaking skills."
- Measurable Objective: "I want to be able to deliver a 10-minute presentation without using notes."

Tip: Identify quantifiable progress indicators, such as numbers, percentages, or other objective measurements.

Achievable: Your goal should be realistic and achievable, considering your resources, constraints, and current circumstances. Setting too ambitious a target may lead to frustration or demotivation; however, they should also be challenging enough for you to stay engaged and foster growth.

Example:

- Unrealistic goal: "I want to become fluent in Spanish within one month."
- Achievable goal: "I plan on finishing a beginner's Spanish course within three months."

Tip: Assess your current situation and resources (time, money, skills) to decide if this goal is achievable.

Relevant: Your goal should align with your values, aspirations, and priorities. Relevant goals will keep you motivated and committed in the long run.

Example:

- Irrelevant Goal: "I want to learn advanced calculus" (if there is no personal or professional interest in mathematics).
- Relevant Goal: "I want to learn basic accounting principles" (if you're an entrepreneur managing your business finances).

Tip: Reflect on long-term objectives and values to make the goal meaningful and applicable in your life.

Time-bound: Set a specific deadline or time frame for completing your goal. This creates urgency and motivates you to stay focused and dedicated. Your timeline could include short-term milestones as well as long-term targets.

Example:

- Open-ended goal: "I want to write a novel."
- Time-bound Goal: "I want to finish writing the first draft of a 50,000-word novel within six months."

Tip: Set realistic but challenging deadlines to stay motivated and keep moving toward your objective.

By using SMART criteria to craft your goals, you can increase the likelihood of reaching them and stay motivated throughout the process. Be sure to assess progress regularly and adjust goals according to changes in circumstances or priorities.

Break Down Your Goals into Smaller Steps

At times, large goals may seem too intimidating to tackle, leading to procrastination or avoidance. Breaking them down into manageable chunks helps make them more achievable and helps maintain motivation levels.

Example: If your goal is to write a book, break it down into smaller steps like creating an outline, researching, writing a specific number of words daily, and setting deadlines for each chapter. (That's exactly how I finally managed to get this book out of my head and into print despite my procrastination issues!)

Prioritize Your Goals

Prioritizing your goals is critical for focusing your efforts on what matters most and making the most efficient use of time and resources. !

Here are some strategies for prioritizing your goals:

1. Align with values and long-term objectives: Make sure your goals align with your core values and contribute to your long-term vision. Prioritize those which have the greatest effect on personal or professional growth.

Example: If your long-term objective is to have a successful career in marketing, prioritize goals related to developing marketing skills and gaining industry experience.

Tip: Consider your values, interests, and long-term aspirations when selecting which goals are most pertinent and essential to you in life.

2. Evaluate time sensitivity when prioritizing goals based on deadlines: Prioritize tasks according to their urgency or external factors that could impact their completion date.

Example: If you have a certification exam due in three months, prioritize studying for it over starting a new hobby.

Tip: Use a calendar or planner to keep track of important dates and deadlines, then regularly review your goals to ensure urgent tasks are addressed first.

3. Evaluate Potential Benefits/Impact: Prioritize goals according to any potential benefits they may have on your life or career.

Example: If learning a new language could significantly boost your job prospects, prioritize this goal over other less important ones.

Tip: Make a list of potential benefits for each goal and compare them against one another to decide which should be given priority.

4. Align Short-term and Long-Term Goals: Create a balance between short-term and long-term objectives to stay motivated and make steady progress toward your overall objectives.

Example: Prioritize short-term goals like finishing a project at work alongside long-term ones such as earning a degree or saving for a house.

Tip: Create a timeline that includes both short-term and long-term objectives, then use this plan to prioritize your tasks and allocate your time/resources efficiently.

5. Utilize a Prioritization Matrix: A prioritization matrix can help you objectively assess and compare your goals based on urgency, impact, and effort.

Example: Create a matrix that ranks goals on a scale of 1-10 based on factors like importance, urgency, and effort required. Goals with higher scores should be prioritized.

Tip: Customize your prioritization matrix to include factors pertinent to your objectives and circumstances.

These strategies can help you prioritize your goals and focus on what matters most. Regularly review and adjust your priorities according to changes in life, progress toward those objectives, as well as new opportunities that arise.

Set Realistic Deadlines

Deadlines can be an effective motivator, but they should also be realistic. Setting unrealistic deadlines may lead to feelings of failure and demotivation.

Example: When learning a new language, consider how much time you can commit daily and how long it typically takes to become fluent, then set an achievable deadline accordingly.

Monitor Your Progress

Monitor your progress regularly to stay motivated and make adjustments as needed. Reminisce on accomplishments and celebrate small victories to stay motivated. This can help keep motivation levels high during difficult times.

Example: If you want to save money, watch your savings account balance and celebrate when you reach certain milestones, such as saving $1,000.

Stay Flexible and Adapt

Life can be unpredictable, sometimes necessitating you to adjust your goals according to new circumstances. Be open to reevaluating these objectives and making necessary modifications as needed.

Example: If you're injured and can't exercise for a few weeks, adjust your fitness goals by focusing on other aspects such as physical therapy, nutrition, or mental wellness.

By following these guidelines, you'll be well on your way to set meaningful goals that will bring about positive changes and give your life direction. Like any other skill, practice makes perfect and pays off; remain patient, persistent, and flexible - you might find yourself achieving more than ever imagined possible!

Putting it All Together

Values are the guiding principles that guide your decisions and actions, while goals represent specific objectives you wish to accomplish. Aligning your values, needs, passions, and goals can help create a life more in tune with yourself and navigate challenges that may arise as we adapt to an ever-changing world.

Here are some tips for using what we have covered in this chapter to find purpose and shape one's direction:

1. Reflect on Your Needs and Values: Take some time out of your busy day to reflect on what truly matters to you. Consider prioritizing areas such as personal growth, relationships, career, health, and community; you could even think about qualities in others that you admire and the kind of person you aspire to become.

2. Create a List of Your Core Values: List values that resonate with you. Some examples include honesty, compassion, family, creativity, freedom, and growth. Aim to identify 5-10 core values that represent your guiding principles.

3. Prioritize Your Needs and Values: Consider the significance of each need and value on your list and rank them according to importance. Doing this will enable you to identify which values and needs are most important to you, guiding decision-making and goal-setting processes.

4. Assess Your Current Alignment With Values and Needs: Take stock of your life and evaluate whether your actions, decisions, and commitments align with your values and meet your needs. If some areas are out of sync, consider making changes

that would align them.

5. Identify Your Long and Short-Term Goals: Starting with your needs and values in mind, create a list of long-term (e.g., 5-10 years) and short-term objectives (e.g., one year) that reflect your priorities and desired direction in life. Your targets should be specific, measurable, achievable, relevant, and time-bound (SMART).

6. Break Down Your Goals into Smaller Objectives: Break your goals into more manageable chunks to stay motivated and focused on progressing. Doing this simplifies tracking achievements and maintaining momentum as you work towards larger aims.

7. Create an action plan: Construct a strategy that outlines the steps you need to take to meet your objectives, including any resources, support systems, or learning opportunities necessary. Set deadlines for each step so that you remain accountable and maintain forward momentum.

8. Review and adjust Your Goals Regularly: As you grow and develop, so will your values, needs, and goals. Regularly revisit these to ensure they reflect what you desire for the future. Make necessary adjustments to keep on track while maintaining a sense of direction and purpose.

This practice not only helps you navigate change and uncertainty but also allows for living in alignment with yourself, making more deliberate choices, and stimulating personal growth.

CHAPTER FIVE

Building Resilience in a Changing Landscape

So far we have covered how to find purpose and set direction. Now it is time to discuss how to navigate the challenges that threaten to knock us off course. However, it is important to keep in mind that sometimes life changes may shift our priorities and so, learning to adapt to change and reorient oneself is a critical life skill. We call that skill "resilience." In a world that is rapidly evolving, particularly in the post-pandemic and post-AI era, developing resilience is crucial for adapting and thriving amidst constant change.

What is Resilience?

Resiliency is the ability to adapt, persevere, and recover from setbacks, challenges, and adversity, maintaining mental and emotional well-being in the process. Resilient people can cope with changes, learn from failures, and transform negative experiences into opportunities for growth and self-improvement. In essence, resilience is the capacity to withstand and rebound from life's challenges, enabling one to navigate through life with strength, flexibility, and optimism.

Developing resilience offers numerous benefits that contribute to improving one's mental, emotional, and physical well-being. Some key benefits of resilience include:

1. Ability to better cope with stress: Resilient individuals can

better manage and adapt to stressful situations, in turn reducing the negative impact of stress on their mental and physical health.

2. Faster recovery from adversity: Resilient people tend to bounce back more quickly from setbacks, disappointments, or failures, enabling them to return to a normal, functioning state sooner.

3. Increased emotional intelligence: Building resilience often involves developing greater self-awareness, empathy, and effective communication skills, which can lead to healthier relationships.

4. Improved problem-solving skills: Resilient individuals are more likely to approach challenges with a solution-focused mindset, thus enabling them to identify and implement effective strategies for overcoming obstacles.

5. Greater self-confidence: As one develops resiliency, their positive experiences facing and overcoming previous challenges will contribute to increased self-esteem and self-confidence.

6. Better mental health: By more effectively navigating life's challenges, resilient individuals tend to have lower rates of stress, depression, anxiety, and other related mental health issues.

7. Enhanced physical health: Chronic stress leads to physical illness, so improving one's ability to effectively cope with stress can have a positive impact on physical health by reducing the risk of stress-related illnesses and promoting healthy behaviors, such as regular exercise and proper nutrition.

8. Greater life satisfaction: Resilient people are more likely to experience a sense of purpose and satisfaction in life since they can face adversity with a positive outlook and continue to pursue their goals and dreams.

9. Increased personal growth: By facing and overcoming challenges, and viewing challenges as opportunities for learning and self-improvement, one will improve one's capacity for personal growth, self-discovery, and the development of new skills, abilities, and perspectives.

10. Career perks: Resiliency enables one to adapt to and navigate changes in job markets, emerging technologies, and societal transformations that can impact one's career.

By developing resilience, we can navigate the challenges of this rapidly changing world with greater confidence and grace, fostering increased well-being and personal growth.

Tips for Building Resiliency

Consider adopting these strategies to build resilience and thrive in an ever-changing world. We have already begun exploring some of these, with more detailed discussions throughout this book to come.

Embody Change and Uncertainty

One key ingredient for resilience is the courage to embrace change and uncertainty. Instead of resisting or fearing change, view it as an opportunity for growth and learning. By having a flexible mindset, you'll be better equipped to navigate changes in the environment and seize new opportunities. (We will cover a growth mindset in Part 2)

Example: When AI automates a graphic designer's job, she embraces the change by upskilling and learning new software. This enables her to transition into a more specialized and in-demand role within her industry.

Establish a Strong Support Network

Social support is an integral factor in developing resilience, as it helps us cope with stress, creates a sense of belongingness, and offers invaluable resources and encouragement. A strong support network can provide emotional and practical comfort as you adjust to change. Foster healthy connections with friends, family members, colleagues, and mentors who can offer comfort, advice, and assistance during times of transition. Strive for opportunities to connect with others. Take part in social activities, join clubs or organizations, or volunteer your time to build your support system. Furthermore, be willing to ask for help when needed and offer it back, as this can strengthen bonds and foster a sense of community.

Example: A recent college graduate struggling to find work in his chosen field turns to his network of professors, classmates, and alums for job leads, advice, and moral support.

Focus on personal growth and continuous learning.

Commit to lifelong learning as an investment in yourself. Stay current in your field, pursue new interests, and explore personal and professional development opportunities. Education should boost resilience and make you a more desirable candidate in the job market.

Example: A marketing manager enrolls in online courses to stay abreast of the newest digital marketing and social media trends, ensuring she remains current with industry changes and is well-equipped to tackle new challenges.

Nurturing a Growth Mindset is essential in this endeavor. A growth mindset is a belief that our abilities, intelligence, and talents can be enhanced and developed through dedication and hard work. Cultivating such an attitude will increase resilience by helping us view challenges as learning opportunities rather than insurmountable obstacles. Embracing setbacks as learning experiences and focusing on the process of improvement rather than the end result are key ingredients for successful growth.

In our upcoming chapter, we'll dive deep into the importance of cultivating a growth mindset.

Practice Self-care and Stress Management

Staying mentally and emotionally balanced is critical to building resilience in today's changing landscape. Indulge in relaxing practices such as meditation, spending time outdoors, or engaging in hobbies that bring you joy. Balance your lifestyle by prioritizing exercise, sleep, and nutrition. Mindful coping strategies from self-care practices can increase resilience by helping us better manage stress and overcome challenges. Avoid harmful coping mechanisms like substance abuse problems, poor eating habits, or excessive screen time, which exacerbate stress and hinder personal growth.

Example: A successful entrepreneur begins each day with 15 minutes of meditation to manage stress and maintain a positive outlook, even when faced with unexpected obstacles.

Be Proactive

Instead of waiting for change to come your way, take control and shape it yourself. Monitor emerging trends, anticipate potential difficulties, and take steps to prepare yourself now for what lies ahead.

Example: An IT professional, anticipating the rise of AI and automation, begins learning programming languages relevant to AI development. By doing so, they position themselves for future job openings within this field while becoming more productive at their current job.

Develop a Sense of Purpose

A strong sense of purpose can provide motivation and direction during times of transition. Reflect on your interests, values, passions, and long-term objectives, and use these insights to guide decisions and actions.

Example: A non-profit worker passionate about environmental conservation chooses to pivot her career toward renewable energy, aligning it with her values and providing her work with a sense of meaning.

Learning From Setbacks and Failures

Setbacks and failures are part of life; embrace them as opportunities for learning and growth, then use what you've learned to make better decisions moving forward.

Example: A business owner whose initial venture fails takes the time to analyze why and applies this knowledge when launching a new, more successful venture.

Cultivate optimism and a positive mindset.

Positivity is essential for building resilience when facing change. Focus on the good things in your life, and surround yourself with upbeat people who share this outlook.

Example: An employee laid off due to company restructuring chooses to view the situation as an opportunity to explore new career paths and acquire new skills rather than dwelling on its negative aspects.

Practice Effective Communication

Effective communication is essential for building resilience, allowing you to express your thoughts, feelings, and needs clearly and assertively. This ability can help you navigate difficult conversations, maintain healthy relationships and boundaries, and advocate for yourself during times of change.

Example: A project manager facing a tight deadline communicates her worries to her team and supervisor, enabling them to work together and find an amicable resolution that benefits all involved.

Embrace Adaptability and Problem-Solving

Develop adaptability and problem-solving skills to better deal with unexpected obstacles, building confidence in handling any situation. Develop a flexible mindset, think creatively, and approach obstacles with a solution-oriented attitude. Practice accepting change as an opportunity for growth and learning; strengthen problem-solving techniques while being open to exploring alternative approaches when faced with difficulties.

Ex: When a small business owner experiences supply chain disruptions due to global events, she quickly adjusts by finding alternative suppliers and altering her product offerings to minimize the negative impact on her operations.

Build Financial Resilience

Financial resilience is the capacity to manage and recover from economic setbacks. Having a safety net can offer peace of mind and enable you to navigate career changes more confidently.

Tips for building financial resilience may include:
- Establishing an emergency fund to cover unexpected expenses
- Reducing debt and managing credit responsibly
- Diversifying income sources through side hustles or investments

Example: An independent contractor facing a sudden decline in work can rely on his emergency fund and income from a side gig to remain financially secure during the downturn.

Seek Feedback and Mentorship

Actively seek feedback and mentorship from others to accelerate your personal and professional growth. Constructive criticism can help you identify areas for improvement, while mentoring provides invaluable guidance as you navigate a rapidly-changing landscape.

Example: An ambitious entrepreneur seeks the advice of an experienced business owner to gain valuable insights into practical strategies for running a successful startup in today's competitive market.

Foster a Sense of Humor

Maintaining a sense of humor can help one cope with stress, keep perspective, and find joy even in stressful situations. Studies have demonstrated that laughter has numerous mental and physical health advantages, making it an invaluable asset in building resilience.

Example: A team leader uses humor to lift the spirit during a particularly challenging project, helping boost team morale and reduce stress levels.

Practice Self-Compassion

Self-compassion refers to the kindness, understanding, and acceptance we extend ourselves during trying times. By practicing self-compassion, we can build resilience by developing a healthier relationship with ourselves that provides comfort and support.

Here are some tips to help you cultivate self-compassion:

1. Alter Your Speaking Patterns: Pay attention to how you speak to yourself in difficult moments or when making mistakes. Replace negative self-talk with kind, understanding language - like speaking it to a friend or loved one.
2. Common humanity: Recognize that everyone occasionally experiences setbacks, failures, and imperfections. Recognizing these events as part of life can help foster self-compassion and reduce feelings of isolation.
3. Practice self-kindness: Be kind to yourself, allow yourself to make mistakes, experience emotions, and ask for help when needed. Prioritize self-care activities that nourish your mental, emotional, and physical well-being. Show yourself the same understanding and support you would extend to a loved one; show yourself patience during difficult times.

4. Reflect on Your Accomplishments: Regularly celebrate and appreciate your successes and positive qualities. Doing this helps maintain an objective perspective of yourself and promotes self-compassion.

5. Set Realistic Expectations: Recognize your limitations and avoid setting unrealistic goals or expectations for yourself. Acknowledge that nobody is perfect, so accepting your shortcomings and drawing inspiration from them is essential.

Example: After weeks of hard work on a project, only to have it rejected by your supervisor, you might experience disappointment, frustration, and self-doubt. Instead of suppressing or avoiding these emotions, take a moment to acknowledge and validate them. Recognize that it's normal to experience feelings such as these after experiencing a setback.

Part 2

Personal Development

CHAPTER SIX

Nurturing a Growth Mindset

At its core, a growth mindset is an idea that our abilities, intelligence, and skills can be improved over time through hard work, dedication, and enthusiasm for learning rather than being hardwired for innate talent. This concept was first popularized by psychologist Carol Dweck who observed two types of people: those with a growth mindset and those with fixed mindsets.

Contrary to a fixed mindset, which holds that qualities cannot be changed, a growth mindset encourages individuals to view obstacles as opportunities for personal improvement and growth. This outlook promotes enthusiasm for learning and resilience when faced with hardship - essential qualities needed for achieving success and personal fulfillment.

This chapter will focus on cultivating a growth mindset which we touched on in part one. We'll explore the key characteristics of a growth mindset, such as accepting failure, cultivating curiosity, seeking feedback, and adopting a flexible attitude. These skills will support you as you determine your purpose and forge your own path through life. While part one answers the question of how one finds one's way, this and the remaining parts of the book cover how one remains on course during that journey, especially during stormy weather.

Here are some key characteristics of a growth mindset:

1. Accepting Challenges with Open Arms: People with this outlook view challenges as opportunities to learn and grow

rather than insurmountable obstacles. They don't fear taking risks because they understand that true progress often requires pushing boundaries and facing difficulties head-on.

2. Persistence and Resilience: A growth mindset promotes perseverance, as individuals understand that learning and improvement take time and effort. They are more likely to recover from setbacks and keep working toward their objectives, viewing failures as valuable feedback in the growth process.

3. Lifelong Learning: People with a growth mindset are curious and eager to learn new things since they understand that knowledge and skills can continually be enhanced. They actively seek opportunities for personal and professional growth, making them more likely to remain lifelong learners.

4. The Strength of Effort: A growth mindset recognizes and values hard work in achieving success. Individuals with this outlook believe they can develop their abilities through dedication, practice, and perseverance; therefore, they are more motivated to put in extra effort to reach their objectives.

5. Seeking Feedback and Learning From Criticism: Those with a growth mindset value constructive criticism, as it helps them identify areas for improvement and development. They tend not to take criticism personally and are more open to learning from mistakes.

By adopting this mindset, we can transform how we respond to challenges and setbacks, creating the conditions for success and personal development in all areas of our lives.

Fail Gloriously

Benjamin Franklin once said, "...*In this world, nothing can be said to be certain, except death and taxes.*" He missed one... *failure.*

When I had just started learning piano, every time I made a mistake while playing a piece, I would stop and replay that part, or worse, start over from the beginning. It made me very shy to play in public since I did not want people to hear my mistakes. Each time I corrected myself, my teacher reminded me to keep going. Eventually, his frustration began to show, and he elaborated on why he was pushing me to continue through my errors. I was on guard for my mistakes, so I was not playing from the heart. On top of that, by correcting my mistakes, I broke the timing of the music and thus brought attention to my errors. He explained that when you commit yourself to playing the piece through, you allow yourself the freedom to experience the music and play with feeling. When we keep to the timing, people are less likely to notice the error or quickly forget about it since they enjoyed listening to the music and were focused on following the piece, not stopping to analyze it along the way. The flow moves the listener along. Since then, I have found this logic can be applied anywhere one is learning a new skill, whether in the dojo or a new language.

No one likes making mistakes or appearing less than perfect, but try as we may; we will stumble. The desire to look perfect and professional can stifle our authenticity and the risk-taking needed for success. When I began my journey as a transformational coach and working on my certification, I was very worried my practice partners would notice when I was unsure how to proceed during a practice session. Only when I owned my insecurity and even shared what I felt with my partners could I connect with them on a more personal level. Trust in a coaching session comes not from presenting oneself as perfect but by being open and authentic. If I make a mistake or say something that was taken offensively, I own it and move forward. My clients will generally feel encouraged to follow my lead, and the coaching relationship will strengthen.

Failure will be your inevitable companion if you are truly living your life. Instead of fearing or avoiding failure, view it as an opportunity to learn and improve. Recognizing that failure is an essential part of the learning process can help you overcome setbacks and achieve your goals while building resilience.

Our successes are built upon the solid foundations of our failures. When learning something new, we first suck (hence why you are learning it), and through practice, we eventually make progress - we suck less and less. In the dojo, my sensei once told me (as I was splattered on the mat) it's not about winning - it's about "dying" less. Behind every success story are a myriad of necessary failures and bad decisions. Those blunders tend to get edited out of the biographies unless they can be spun to make for a good story.

Here are some strategies for accepting failure as part of your journey toward cultivating a growth mindset:

1. Reframe Your Perspective on Failure: Rather than seeing failure as a negative outcome, view it as an invaluable chance to learn and grow. Remember that everyone experiences failure at some point in their personal or professional development journey; accept failure as an inevitable part of this process for all of us.

2. Analyze Your Failures: After experiencing a setback, reflect and identify what went wrong. By understanding the causes, you can create strategies to prevent repeating similar errors in the future.

3. Focus on Lessons Learned: Instead of dwelling on the failure itself, take note of the lessons it offers. Recognize and apply the knowledge and skills you've acquired from this experience to improve your approach in future endeavors.

4. Develop Resilience: Accepting failure helps you build resilience, allowing you to recover faster from setbacks and maintain a positive outlook. Practice perseverance and keep an optimistic attitude even when faced with difficulties.

5. Cultivate a growth mindset: A growth mindset is a belief that your abilities and intelligence can be enhanced through hard work, effort, and learning from mistakes. Foster this attitude by accepting challenges, persisting despite difficulties, and viewing failure as an opportunity for development.

6. Seek Feedback and Constructive Criticism: Actively seek feedback from others to gain insights into areas where you can improve. Accept constructive criticism as a tool for growth, and use it to make necessary adjustments in your approach.

7. Set Achievable Expectations: While setting ambitious goals is important, setting realistic expectations is also essential. Recognize that failure is part of the process, and you may experience setbacks.

8. Practice Self-Compassion: Show yourself kindness and understanding when you fail. Acknowledge that everyone makes mistakes, and treat yourself with the same understanding and compassion you would offer a friend in

similar circumstances.

9. Maintain a Positive Attitude: Focus on the positives in your life and remain optimistic, even when faced with failure. A positive outlook will help you stay motivated to keep working toward your goals despite setbacks.

10. Share Your Experiences With Others: Talking about failure with others can help normalize the experience and create a supportive atmosphere for growth. Have open discussions about failure with friends, family members, or colleagues so that you can learn from each other and foster an atmosphere of learning and development.

Finally, accept responsibility! Excuses and passing blame rob you of any benefit to be gained from one's mistakes or setbacks. Face reality head-on, learn what you can, and move on - remembering that failure does not define who you are or your potential. Instead, it serves as an opportunity to grow, adapt, and become a stronger, more capable individual.

As actor Cate Blanchett once said (in one of my favorite quotes of all time), *"If you know you are going to fail, then fail gloriously."*

The Power of Vulnerability

Vulnerability gets a bad rap, often associated with weakness or fear. However, it can also be a remarkably transformative force in our lives. Embracing vulnerability allows us to connect more deeply with ourselves and others, fostering personal growth, resilience, and authentic relationships.

Here's how the power of vulnerability can positively impact various aspects of our lives:

1. Authentic connections: Vulnerability is the key to building meaningful relationships. By allowing ourselves to be seen, we create opportunities for others to connect with us on a deeper level. Sharing our fears, dreams, and emotions creates an environment of trust and understanding, strengthening the bonds we share with others.

2. Personal growth: When we face our vulnerabilities, we gain a deeper understanding of ourselves, our strengths, and our

weaknesses. This self-awareness allows us to grow and develop as individuals. Embracing vulnerability pushes us out of our comfort zones, helping us build resilience and adaptability in the face of challenges.

3. Empathy and compassion: By recognizing and embracing our vulnerabilities, we can better understand and empathize with the struggles and challenges others face. This empathy can foster compassion, kindness, and support, not only for ourselves but also for those around us.

4. Creativity and innovation: Vulnerability involves taking risks and being open to the possibility of failure. This willingness to explore new ideas and face potential setbacks is essential for creativity and innovation. Embracing vulnerability in our work or artistic pursuits can lead to breakthroughs, originality, and growth.

5. Emotional well-being: When we allow ourselves to be vulnerable, we permit ourselves to experience a full range of positive and negative emotions. This emotional authenticity is crucial for our mental health and well-being. Suppressing emotions or hiding our true selves can contribute to stress, anxiety, and other mental health issues.

6. Enhancing self-compassion: By acknowledging our vulnerabilities, we can cultivate self-compassion and self-kindness, recognizing that imperfection is a natural part of the human experience. This self-compassion can reduce self-criticism and improve our overall sense of self-worth.

7. Building trust and collaboration: In team environments, vulnerability is critical in establishing trust and fostering collaboration. When leaders and team members are willing to be vulnerable, they create an atmosphere of openness, honesty, and shared responsibility, resulting in more effective teamwork and problem-solving.

As with failure, vulnerability is not a sign of weakness but rather a testament to our strength and humanity.

Cultivating Curiosity

Curiosity fosters a growth mindset by inspiring one to explore new ideas, ask questions, and seek knowledge. It breaks the mind out of passivity, adding depth to our lives by searching for the answers to our questions. A curious mind is more observant of new ideas, opportunities, and inspiration, opening up new worlds and possibilities normally not visible because they are hidden behind the surface of everyday, unquestioned life. The more questions one asks, the more the universe unfolds in its vastness. Every minor detail has stories to tell. While guiding a Forest Therapy session during the pandemic, where my clients felt disconnected from the world due to mask-wearing and social distancing, I handed out small magnifying glasses. I invited them to spread out and observe the world through that lens. People were amazed at the complex and beautiful world around them, which usually goes unseen. Mini forests and creatures, dazzling patterns teased of a far more varied and beautiful world than we had considered. What other mysteries are right before us, merely waiting for a curious mind to notice?

Be open to new experiences and challenge your assumptions and beliefs. Indulge in activities that pique your interest, such as reading books, attending workshops, or joining interest groups. By cultivating curiosity, you'll broaden your horizons and unlock your full potential.

Here are some strategies for cultivating curiosity:

1. Embrace the Unknown: Challenge yourself to step outside your comfort zone and explore new ideas, experiences, and perspectives. Accepting that nothing is certain in life opens you up to learning and personal growth opportunities.

2. Ask open-ended Questions: Develop the habit of asking thoughtful, exploratory questions to encourage exploration and critical thinking. Instead of looking for quick solutions, dig deeper into topics to gain greater insight and appreciation for them.

3. Be an Active Listener: Active listening is key when engaging with others, allowing you to absorb new information and ideas. Be open to learning from others' experiences and perspectives, even if they differ from your own.

4. Pursue Your Interests: Follow your passions and interests, and explore topics or activities that pique your curiosity. Doing this may uncover new talents, acquire new skills, and gain a

better insight into the world around you.

5. Adopt a beginner's mindset: Approach new topics and experiences with the humility and curiosity of someone just starting. Remember that there is always more to learn, even in areas where you feel knowledgeable.

6. Seek Diverse Experiences: Expand your worldview by engaging with diverse people, cultures, and ideas to deepen your understanding of the world and challenge your assumptions. Engaging with different viewpoints can foster creativity and spark your interest in exploring new things.

7. Reflect on Your Learning: Take time to pause and consider what you have learned, how it has shaped your understanding, and how it can be applied in future scenarios.

8. Encourage Curiosity in Others: Foster an atmosphere that promotes inquiry and learning for yourself and those around you. Share your findings, ask questions, and have open, thought-provoking discussions.

9. Stay Open to Change: Be willing and adaptable when presented with new information or experiences. Recognize that our world is constantly in flux, so keep an open mind to stay agile and responsive to new opportunities. Challenge your assumptions!

10. Be Patient and Persistent: Fostering curiosity requires patience and perseverance. Acknowledge that cultivating curiosity is an ongoing journey that requires patience and determination. Take on challenges head-on, remain resilient in the face of setbacks, and view setbacks as opportunities for growth and learning.

Seeking Feedback

Constructive feedback is invaluable for personal and professional growth, providing insights into one's strengths and areas for improvement. We all have our blind spots and biases, which will limit our perception and box in our thinking. While self-reflection can help, the greatest tool is gaining an outside perspective through the observations and feedback of others.

Actively seek feedback from others such as mentors, colleagues, friends, or family members; be open to criticism and use it as an opportunity to learn and improve yourself; then implement the suggestions given and constantly strive to improve yourself.

Here are some strategies for seeking feedback to promote a growth mindset:

1. Accept Feedback as a Learning Opportunity: Take feedback with an open mind, seeing it as an opportunity to grow and improve. Accept that constructive criticism is part of growth and development - not a personal attack.

2. Request Feedback Regularly: Be proactive about seeking feedback from peers, colleagues, supervisors, friends, or family members. Regular feedback can help you recognize patterns, monitor progress, and adjust your approach.

3. Be Specific in Your Feedback Requests: When asking for feedback, focus on specific areas or aspects where you would like to improve. This allows others to provide more tailored and practical advice and will enable you to focus on addressing those issues effectively.

4. Create a safe environment for feedback: Foster open and honest communication by creating a nonjudgmental space to receive input. Show others you value their opinion and are genuinely interested in their viewpoint.

5. Practice active listening: When receiving feedback, listen carefully and attentively without interrupting or becoming defensive. Ask questions to clarify any points or suggestions made, and express your appreciation for the insight shared.

6. Reflect on the Feedback: After receiving feedback, ponder its meaning and implications. Determine which aspects are most helpful and pertinent for your growth, then create an action plan to address those areas.

7. Implement the Feedback: Put the feedback you've been given into action by changing your approach, behavior, or strategies. Track your progress and continue seeking feedback for confirmation that you are progressing in the right direction.

8. Be Open to Diverse Opinions: Seek feedback from individuals with various backgrounds, experiences, and expertise. Doing this can give you a deeper insight into your strengths and

areas for improvement.

9. Master how to manage negative feedback: Though constructive criticism can be helpful and insightful, it's essential to learn how to handle negative feedback that may not be useful or relevant. Consider the source, context, and validity of any feedback you receive before focusing on its beneficial aspects for growth.

10. Offer Feedback to Others: Take part in a feedback exchange by offering your insights and constructive criticism. Not only does this promote their growth, but it also helps them hone their communication skills and empathic understanding.

Any time you experience an intense emotional reaction to feedback, take that as a sign that there is something valuable to learn there. Perhaps challenging certain assumptions and beliefs has opened up new avenues of insight. Consider what the perceived threat or offense was.

Adopting a Lifelong Learning Attitude

A growth mindset is founded on the idea that learning should be an ongoing endeavor. Make time to acquire new skills, expand your knowledge, and stay informed about your environment. Take advantage of new learning opportunities like online courses, workshops, or certifications relevant to your interests and objectives by adopting a lifelong learning attitude. With such a mindset in place, you'll be better equipped to tackle challenges as they come your way.

Here are some strategies for cultivating a lifelong learning attitude:

1. Cultivate Curiosity: Foster an attitude of open-mindedness about the world around you by asking questions and seeking to comprehend new ideas and perspectives. Curiosity fosters learning, leading to personal growth and expanded horizons.

2. Stay Open to New Experiences: Be willing to try new activities, connect with new people, and investigate different subjects. Doing so can open you to new ideas, perspectives, and learning opportunities.

3. Embrace Challenge: See challenges as opportunities for growth and learning rather than obstacles that must be

avoided. Accepting difficulties can build resilience, enhance problem-solving abilities, and give you a sense of gratification at the end of it all.

4. Engage in Continuous Self-Reflection: Regularly reflect on your experiences, knowledge, and skills. Consider what has been learned, how it has shaped your understanding, and how it can be applied to future situations.

5. Create Personal Learning Goals: Set personal and professional growth objectives, then commit to achieving them. Achieving these milestones can give you direction, drive motivation, and a sense of gratification as you advance your learning journey.

6. Pursue Diverse Learning Opportunities: Take advantage of various learning opportunities, such as online courses, workshops, seminars, books, YouTube videos, etc., to expand your knowledge and develop new skills. Staying engaged through diverse experiences will motivate you to reach new heights in personal growth.

7. Learn from Others: Appreciate the value of learning from those around you, regardless of background, age, or expertise. Be receptive to their opinions and engage in meaningful conversations to deepen your understanding.

8. Apply Your Learning: Use the knowledge and skills you've acquired in personal and professional situations. Doing so can deepen your comprehension, offering further growth opportunities.

9. Stay Adaptable and Flexible: Be open to change and adjust your approach, opinions, or beliefs according to new knowledge or experiences. Lifelong learning necessitates adaptability and flexibility in light of evolving circumstances.

10. Share Your Knowledge: Pass on your learning by engaging in collaborative learning experiences. Doing so can deepen your comprehension, develop communication skills, and contribute to the growth of others.

By cultivating a lifelong learning mindset, you can develop an attitude of continuous improvement that encourages personal development and adaptability. Accept learning as an ever-evolving journey that enriches your life and deepens your comprehension of the world. Be patient with yourself as you explore all opportunities to grow, thrive, and understand more deeply.

Celebrating Success

In our fast-paced world, it's easy to overlook the value of celebrating one's achievements, both big and small. However, taking the time to acknowledge and celebrate one's successes is essential for our well-being and supports the development of a growth mindset.

Below are some reasons why acknowledging and celebrating one's success is so important:

1. Boosts motivation and confidence: Celebrating your achievements can provide a sense of accomplishment and self-worth, boosting your motivation and self-confidence. Recognizing your progress and abilities can empower you to continue pursuing your goals and face new challenges with enthusiasm.

2. Enhances gratitude and positivity: Acknowledging your successes helps you cultivate gratitude for your abilities, opportunities, and support from others. This positive mindset can improve your overall happiness and well-being, making it easier to maintain a balanced perspective in the face of adversity.

3. Promotes personal growth: Reflecting on your accomplishments allows you to identify your strengths, areas of improvement, and the factors that contributed to your success. This self-awareness is essential for personal growth and development, enabling you to set more meaningful goals and work towards becoming the best version of yourself.

4. Encourages a healthy work-life balance: Celebrating your successes can help you establish a more balanced lifestyle by reminding you to pause, reflect, and enjoy the fruits of your labor. Taking the time to relax and savor your achievements can prevent burnout and foster a healthier relationship with work and personal life.

5. Strengthens social connections: Sharing your successes with friends, family, and colleagues creates opportunities for fellowship, support, and mutual celebration. These positive

interactions can strengthen relationships and foster a sense of belonging and camaraderie.

6. Inspires others: Your achievements can be a source of inspiration and motivation for others. Celebrating your successes can show others what is possible and encourage them to pursue their goals and dreams.

7. Reinforces goal-setting habits: Recognizing and celebrating your accomplishments can help reinforce the practice of setting and working towards goals. This ongoing cycle of goal-setting and achievement can lead to a more fulfilling and purpose-driven life.

8. Creates a positive feedback loop: Celebrating your successes can increase motivation, confidence, and satisfaction, which can drive you to achieve even greater accomplishments. This positive feedback loop can result in continuous personal and professional growth.

How one chooses to celebrate one's success is unimportant. What is important is that you acknowledge that success. No success is too small to celebrate. Recognizing and appreciating your achievements can foster a positive mindset, enhance your well-being, and pave the way for continued personal growth and happiness.

Promoting a Growth Mindset

Like any skill, practice makes us more adept at using a growth mindset when we may not be thinking as clearly, such as during a crisis. I am reminded of something my sensei once told me: *Your best in a real fight will be your worst at the dojo.* By this, he meant that in a dojo, which is a supportive environment where no one is trying to harm me, I am not facing significant fear and generally know what to expect from my sparring partners since we are all training on the same moves. In a real fight, we don't know what to expect, and our opponent wants to cause harm. Thus we have to contend with our body's fight or flight response which causes rapid heart rate and tunnel vision. In such a state, we will not remember our fancy moves and instead make do with the basics we have been drilling so long that they are second nature to us. Hence, when things get tough in our lives, we will not likely have the same availability of our skills as we would when relaxed. So the more we practice and hone our skills, the more available they will be when truly needed.

Here are some questions to encourage a growth mindset. By asking these questions and reflecting on one's experiences, you can cultivate an attitude of continuous learning, adaptation, and personal development that promotes continuous learning, transformation, and personal growth. For those who journal (recommended), these are great prompts when facing a challenge.

1. What can I learn from this situation or experience?
2. How can I develop my skills or knowledge in this area?
3. What challenges have I overcome, and what have I learned from them?
4. How can setbacks or failures be seen as opportunities for growth and learning?
5. What strategies or approaches can I try to overcome this obstacle?
6. Who can I enlist guidance, support, or mentorship in this area?
7. How can I break down long-term goals into smaller achievable steps to track my progress more easily?
8. What are some practical ways to respond constructively to criticism or feedback?
9. How can I recognize my big and small successes as milestones on my developmental journey?
10. How can I maintain a positive and proactive attitude despite challenges or setbacks?
11. How can I encourage others to adopt a growth mindset and support their personal development?
12. What resources, such as books, courses, or workshops, can I draw upon to further my knowledge and skillset?
13. How can I remain curious and open-minded to new ideas, perspectives, and experiences?
14. How can I cultivate patience and perseverance in my personal and professional growth journeys?
15. How can I regularly set aside time for self-reflection and evaluation of progress toward my objectives?

CHAPTER SEVEN

Building Confidence and Self-Esteem

Confidence and self-esteem, though related, are distinct concepts that affect an individual's sense of worth and well-being. Confidence refers to one's belief in one's capacity for completing particular tasks or handling certain situations successfully. Confidence is situational, fluctuating according to context or challenge, and formed by past successes and failures. It can be built and strengthened through practice and exposure.

On the other hand, self-esteem is a more comprehensive assessment of one's worthiness that considers all aspects of one's overall sense of value and worthiness. This aspect of someone's self-concept remains stable over time, reflecting their feelings about themselves. Factors like upbringing, social environment, personal values, achievements, and internal factors like self-compassion or self-awareness can influence one's sense of self-worthiness.

Both confidence and self-esteem integrally play a role in personal development and well-being, though they serve different functions. Confidence enables individuals to tackle specific obstacles with assurance, while self-esteem provides a generalized sense of worth, positively affecting mental and emotional health. Cultivating confidence and self-esteem leads to a more resilient, empowered, and fulfilled life.

In this chapter, we'll examine the significance of confidence and self-worth and how to cultivate them by recognizing and challenging our self-limiting beliefs undermining our sense of worth.

* * *

The Importance of Confidence and Self-Esteem

Confidence allows people to tackle challenges confidently, take risks, learn from experiences, and reach success more quickly. Self-esteem motivates individuals, helps them deal with difficult circumstances more successfully, and leads to personal and professional growth. On the other hand, low self-esteem negatively affects an individual's sense of worth and mental and emotional well-being. A healthy sense of self-worth promotes resilience, improved coping skills, and an upbeat outlook on life. It gives individuals the belief in their inherent worth, leading to stronger relationships, wiser decision-making, and a greater sense of fulfillment. In conclusion, confidence and self-esteem are essential in helping individuals lead more fulfilling, empowered lives.

Here are some of the critical roles confidence and self-worth play in our lives:

1. Improved mental health: High self-esteem and confidence are linked to better mental health by decreasing negative self-talk, anxiety, and depression. A positive attitude toward life allows you to approach challenges more optimistically and helps you cope better when faced with them.

2. Enhanced Decision-Making Capacity: With confidence in yourself, you are more likely to trust your judgment and make decisions that align with your values and goals. This can lead to increased satisfaction and success across various aspects of life, such as career, relationships, and personal growth.

3. Greater Resilience: Having healthy self-esteem allows you to recover more quickly from setbacks and failures. When you believe in yourself, challenges become opportunities for growth rather than insurmountable obstacles.

4. Better relationships: Confidence and self-esteem are crucial in developing and maintaining healthy relationships. When you value and respect yourself, you're more likely to set boundaries, communicate clearly, and seek out relationships that offer nurturing support.

5. Higher Motivation and Productivity: A positive sense of self-

worth makes you more likely to pursue your goals with determination and enthusiasm. This can increase motivation and productivity levels, enabling you to accomplish more tasks and find greater fulfillment.

6. Effective Communication: Confident individuals tend to express their thoughts and opinions more openly and assertively. This leads to improved communication, stronger connections, and fruitful collaborations.

7. Reduced Fear of Failure: Having high self-esteem makes you less vulnerable to the fear of failure. Accepting that mistakes may have consequences can encourage you to take calculated risks, seize opportunities, and draw upon past experiences for learning and growth.

8. Enhancing Self-Compassion: Building self-esteem helps you develop greater self-compassion, enabling you to treat yourself with kindness and understanding when faced with difficulties or setbacks. Doing this cultivates a healthier relationship with yourself that promotes personal growth and well-being.

9. Personal Growth and Development: Confidence and self-esteem are crucial for personal development, as they inspire you to try new things, learn from mistakes, and constantly strive for improvement.

10. Greater life satisfaction: Building confidence and self-esteem ultimately leads to a higher sense of overall happiness. When you believe in yourself and your abilities, taking steps toward achieving goals becomes much more accessible - encouraging you to reach for what you want out of life!

Developing Confidence and Self-Esteem

Developing confidence and self-esteem involves cultivating a positive self-image and learning to trust one's abilities and worth. Here are some strategies to help build confidence and self-esteem.

1. Establish achievable, measurable goals so that the sense of accomplishment in achieving those goals can help boost confidence. We discuss how to set such goals in much detail in

Part 1.

2. Practice self-compassion by offering yourself the same support and empathy you would offer a friend.

3. Celebrate achievements: Recognize and celebrate your accomplishments, no matter how small. This helps reinforce your sense of self-worth and builds confidence in your abilities.

4. Focus on strengths: Identify your strengths and talents, and seek opportunities to use and develop them. Focusing on your strengths can help boost self-esteem and foster a more positive self-image. (We'll explore how to identify one's strengths in more detail in Part 4 of this book.)

5. Challenge negative thoughts: Be mindful of negative self-talk and work on reframing these thoughts into more positive and constructive statements. Practicing positive affirmations or journaling about your achievements and qualities can help reinforce a more positive self-image. We'll explore this further later in this chapter.

6. Practice self-care: Maintaining your physical, emotional, and mental well-being is essential for building self-esteem. Engage in activities that make you feel good, such as exercise, hobbies, or spending time with loved ones. Part 3 of this book is dedicated to self-care.

7. Learn from mistakes: Instead of dwelling on failures, view them as learning opportunities. Embrace a growth mindset, recognizing that setbacks can help you grow and improve. We discuss this in more depth at the beginning of Part 2.

8. Develop assertiveness: Practice assertive communication by expressing your needs, desires, and boundaries respectfully and confidently. Assertiveness can help you feel more in control and increase your self-esteem.

9. Surround yourself with positive influences: Cultivate relationships with supportive and uplifting individuals who encourage and inspire you. Positive social connections can help reinforce a healthy self-image and boost self-esteem.

10. Seek professional help if needed: If low confidence or self-esteem is affecting your daily life or mental health, consider seeking the help of a mental health professional who can

provide guidance and support tailored to your specific needs. (I probably sound like a broken record on this point, but it is for a good reason!)

Overcoming Negative Beliefs and Self-talk

Self-limiting beliefs are thoughts we hold about ourselves that undermine our self-worth and limit our potential, keeping us from reaching our goals and living the life we desire. These can become habituated and deeply embedded in our unconscious mind due to past experiences or upbringing. Common examples include feelings of inadequacy, a fear of failure, or believing one doesn't deserve success or happiness. Such beliefs are often manifested through an inner critic.

Challenging self-limiting beliefs is an ongoing journey requiring reflection, dedication, and practice. Once identified, one can work toward dispelling these illusions and realizing one's full potential.

Remember, conquering self-limiting beliefs is a gradual process that takes time and dedication; however, the rewards of this endeavor can be immense and have the power to transform your life for the better.

Though we all struggle with negative beliefs occasionally, the severity of their effects varies. If you're finding it hard to manage daily life due to these beliefs and inner voices, seeking professional assistance for support and understanding is highly recommended.

Here is a general strategy for dealing with negative beliefs and self-talk:

Step 1: Recognize and Understand the Beliefs

The initial step to overcoming self-limiting beliefs and increasing confidence and self-esteem recognizes them. Be mindful of your thoughts, paying attention to recurring patterns or themes that suggest a belief is holding you back. Become aware of that inner critic and any negative self-talk it generates; pay attention when it surfaces and the messages it sends. Journaling is an effective tool for recognizing patterns and tracking progress. Recognizing and confronting one's beliefs will enable you to free yourself from their hold on you, ultimately leading to increased self-assurance.

Given how deeply seated and unconscious our negative thinking can become and how easily we mistake these limiting beliefs for truth, identifying self-limiting beliefs can be a challenge. Here are some strategies that may assist you in recognizing these thoughts:

1. Pay Attention to Your Inner Dialogue: Begin by paying attention to the thoughts that run through your mind throughout the day. When you come across a negative thought or belief, write it down for later review.

2. Identification of the Trigger: Pinpoint the situation or experience that caused you to have a negative thought or belief. Was it an isolated incident, or did it follow a pattern of behavior or specific scenarios?

3. Assess the Source: Consider where your belief originated. Did it come from someone else, such as a parent or teacher? Or has it become something you have internalized from your culture and society?

4. Identification of Impact: Examine how this belief has affected your life. How has it limited you, preventing you from reaching your objectives or living your desired life?

5. Journal: Journaling is an effective tool for uncovering self-limiting beliefs. Write down your thoughts and perceptions about yourself, your abilities, and your limitations. Reflect on how these beliefs might be holding you back or preventing you from reaching your objectives.

6. Be Aware of Patterns: Pay attention to any negative self-talk or beliefs you might have. Are specific situations or circumstances triggering these thoughts, or do these beliefs occur in certain areas of your life, such as relationships or careers? Does the inner critic's voice remind you of someone in your life?

7. Seek Feedback: Seek feedback from others to gain an outside perspective. Ask trusted friends or family members for honest opinions on your strengths and areas for improvement, especially if you are working with a coach or therapist who can offer this valuable assistance.

8. Explore Your Values: Consider what matters most to you and explore your values. Are your beliefs aligned with these? Do your actions reflect these same ideals? Knowing your values

can help clarify priorities and overcome self-limiting beliefs that may conflict with them. What values are these negative beliefs seeking to honor?

9. Be Curious: Approach self-discovery with an attitude of curiosity and openness. Consider different perspectives and possibilities without judgment or criticism of yourself during this process. Ask yourself questions about your beliefs, such as where they came from and how they hold you back, to uncover new insights and possibilities. Use curiosity as fuel for inner exploration!

10. Practice Self-Compassion: Show yourself compassion when confronting self-limiting beliefs. Remember, these ideas may have become deeply embedded due to past experiences, so be kind and gentle with yourself as you work toward changing them.

11. Pay Attention to Emotions: Be mindful of the emotions that arise when confronted with self-limiting beliefs. Commonly, negative emotions like fear, shame, or guilt are associated with these ideas. By identifying and acknowledging these feelings, you can begin working through them and ultimately overcome self-limiting beliefs.

Step 2: Evaluate Your Beliefs

Once we become aware of a limiting belief, exploring its nature and how best to manage it becomes much easier. Before starting this step, be sure you can clearly articulate your negative self-belief. Be as specific as you can in stating the belief and how it manifests in your thoughts, feelings, and actions. This may require returning to step 1 to develop better clarity.

As you evaluate these beliefs, focus on one and find evidence to support or refute that self-limiting belief. Look for examples when the belief has been disproven or contradicted, such as positive feedback from colleagues or promotions in the past. If you believe you cannot succeed in your career, look for signs demonstrating previous success, such as positive feedback from colleagues or promotions.

Are there any facts that support your belief, or is it simply the result of unfounded fears and assumptions? Is the fact that these beliefs have become too big to ignore, or is the fact being exaggerated beyond reason? For instance, perhaps failure has occurred multiple times, and now you feel that success is impossible. Consider alternative explanations or perspectives which could challenge this opinion.

Here is a list of questions you can use during this evaluation process:

1. What is the specific negative self-belief that I hold?
2. What evidence do I have to support this belief?
3. What evidence contradicts or challenges this belief?
4. Is this belief based on facts or assumptions?
5. How does distorted thinking influence this belief?
6. Can I identify a specific event or experience that contributed to the development of this belief?
7. Can I adopt alternative, more positive, or balanced beliefs instead?
8. How does this negative self-belief affect my thoughts, feelings, actions, and overall well-being?
9. What would I say to a friend or loved one who held this same belief about themselves?
10. How might my life be different if I didn't have this negative belief?
11. Is it possible that this belief is only partially true or not accurate at all?
12. What are the potential benefits of challenging and changing this belief?
13. How can I practice self-compassion as I work to evaluate and challenge this belief?
14. Are there any patterns or themes among my negative self-beliefs that I should address?

By reflecting on these questions, you can gain a deeper understanding of these inner saboteurs and begin to challenge their validity. This process can help you develop a more balanced and accurate self-perception, leading to improved self-esteem and overall well-being.

An Alternative Approach to the Inner Critic

While working toward my coaching certification, we were taught an interesting perspective about the inner critic. Instead of viewing it as a malevolent force trying to cause harm and damage, consider it as someone trying to protect or assist you but perhaps not using the healthiest strategy, which ultimately does more harm than good. From this perspective, ask yourself these questions:

- What is the inner critic trying to protect me from or help me with?
- What desires does it wish to fulfill or values does it want to uphold?
- What does the trigger situation look like from its perspective?
- What needs is this critic trying to satisfy?
- If the critic's end game is not to harm, what is truly aiming for? (Consider the discussion in Part 1 about needs vs. strategies and how it may apply to the critic.)

This approach helps identify the source of these beliefs so actions can be taken to soothe your inner critic and silence its voice. For instance, if fear of failure is an unconscious fear within, an inner critic may be that voice telling you you're incapable or ready for success, so it's better to play it safe by not even trying.

I find it helpful to give critics a name, such as "The Douber" or "Nervous Nelson," so you can more quickly recognize and address them when they appear. For instance: "Oh no, there goes Nervous Nelson again - don't worry, Nelson, I got this." Approach these critics with compassion and recognize them for what they indeed are: scared aspects of yourself wanting to help in their flawed way.

Step 3: Take Action

Now that we've identified and understood our limiting belief (an assumption, fear, over-exaggeration, etc.), we can consciously choose how best to counter or transform it. Here are some common methods:

1. Reframe the Belief: Challenge yourself to find a more positive and empowering alternative to self-limiting beliefs. For instance, if you feel that you are unworthy, remind yourself that you are capable and worthy of success; furthermore, adopt an accepting perspective towards negative self-talk such as: instead of saying, "I'm terrible at this," try saying something like: "I'm still learning, and it's okay to make mistakes."

2. Break Down Beliefs: Break down self-limiting beliefs into

smaller components. Identify specific aspects of each belief holding you back and work on challenging each one individually. Breaking up an enormous belief into manageable pieces makes it less overwhelming to manage and less overwhelming overall.

3. Visualize Success: Visualize yourself succeeding despite any self-limiting beliefs you may have. Picture yourself reaching your objectives and living the life you desire.

4. Find Positive Role Models. Find positive role models and surround yourself with supportive and encouraging people. Gain inspiration from others who have overcome difficulties; this will help you realize that you can achieve success.

5. Be defiant: Take steps towards your goals, even small ones. Or set new objectives specifically designed to combat that negative belief. Every journey begins with a tiny step at a time.

6. Utilize Positive Affirmations: Positive affirmations can be an effective tool in challenging self-limiting beliefs. Remind yourself of positive statements about yourself and your abilities, even if you don't fully believe them. With time, these affirmations may reprogram your habitual thinking and alter your perceptions about yourself.

7. Acknowledge the Consequences: Consider how these beliefs might negatively affect your life and relationships. Use this as motivation to challenge these thoughts, creating a more fulfilling and positive lifestyle.

8. Accept the Challenge: My go-to way of challenging a limiting belief is by accepting it as an opportunity. Go ahead - prove them wrong!

9. Experiment with New Behaviors: Challenge your self-limiting beliefs by trying out some new behaviors that go against what you believe. For instance, if you think you're not creative, try engaging in some creative activity and see what happens. Experimenting with different approaches can help challenge those beliefs and broaden your self-concept.

Step 4: Evaluate Progress

Overcoming these limiting beliefs can take time. As you review your progress, consider which steps may need to be revisited. For example, perhaps you find you need to clarify what that belief is (step 1), need to dig deeper into the evaluation process of step 2, or create/revise your action plan in step 3, perhaps adding or revising specific goals.

Celebrate and acknowledge your progress. Overcoming self-limiting beliefs requires time and energy; reward even small victories as steps taken towards conquering them. Focus on achievements no matter how small, and honor both the effort and progress made thus far. Take note of any lessons learned from past setbacks that helped make progress possible.

Lastly, at the risk of being repetitive, a little self-compassion goes a long way here. This is not easy work. The mere fact that you are working through this process begins to lessen the impact of those limiting beliefs. It is much easier to deal with something you know rather than be a slave to unconscious influences. At the very least, you are pulling these inner saboteurs out of the shadows so that you can begin to make more conscious choices in response to their whispers.

Additional Tips

Here are some tips to support you during this process:

1. Practice self-compassion: Show kindness and gentleness toward yourself as you work to overcome self-limiting beliefs. Recognize that changing deeply held beliefs can be challenging, and setbacks are expected as part of the journey.

2. Seek Out Support: Reach out for help from friends, family, or a coach or therapist. Talking with someone you trust about your self-limiting beliefs and your difficulties can help reinforce your efforts while offering new insights. Let them help you see past your blinders.

3. Embrace Discomfort: Accept discomfort as a sign of growth. Challenging self-limiting beliefs can be uncomfortable and may take you outside your comfort zone, but look at these moments as chances for personal development and learning.

4. Focus on Growth Over Perfection: When confronting self-limiting beliefs, emphasize growth rather than perfection. Understand that any progress is worthwhile and celebrate it regardless of size. Adopt a growth mindset and focus on the journey rather than the destination.

5. Practice Gratitude: Express gratitude for the positive things in your life to shift your focus away from self-limiting thoughts and increase your sense of worth. Gratitude can help cultivate a more optimistic outlook and enhance your sense of worth.

6. Keep a Success Journal: Keep track of your successes as you work to overcome self-limiting beliefs. Record all achievements, no matter how small they may seem. Reflect on these triumphs regularly to reinforce your efforts and motivate yourself to keep going.

7. Critics may not leave: Some of our inner critics will stick around for a while, so instead of focusing on removing them, concentrate on learning to recognize and respond to them in ways more aligned with your well-being and success.

CHAPTER EIGHT

The Hero's Journey

The Hero's Journey is an ancient narrative pattern in myths, stories, and legends worldwide. It tells of a hero's journey to overcome challenges and gain wisdom and strength, culminating in their return with newfound knowledge and power. Sounds familiar? Popular films such as Lord of the Rings, Hunger Games, Harry Potter, The Matrix, The Lion King, and Star Wars all present versions of this timeless pattern. Let us say it gets around!

This concept, popularized by American mythologist Joseph Campbell, can provide a valuable framework for cultivating resilience and personal growth.

In this chapter, we will examine the essential elements of the Hero's Journey and consider how they can help you build resilience and personal growth on your journeys.

1. Separation: Leaping Out of One's Comfort Zone

The initial stage of the Hero's Journey calls for the hero to step outside their comfort zone and embark on an exciting new journey, leaving their familiar world behind.

This can be a physical journey, like moving to a new city, or an emotional one, like facing fear. At some point in this stage, there will often be an internal call to adventure and a need to decide whether or not the challenge will be accepted. Sometimes heroes find themselves forced into difficult circumstances but choose instead to take action rather than becoming victims; they have made the conscious decision to venture into unknown territories, embrace change, and take risks.

Lesson:

Resilience and personal growth require us to step outside our comfort zones and embrace change. Whether it's a new job, the end of a relationship, or any other life challenge, these moments of great challenge can be seen as opportunities for growth. By taking risks and facing our fears head-on, we develop the resilience necessary to adapt to new circumstances and overcome challenges.

Tip:

Review your life and identify areas that need improvement or development. Pay attention to recurring thoughts, dreams, or situations that indicate personal growth opportunities.

Example: Have you constantly desired to start your own business but have been held back by fear or self-doubt? Now may be the time for adventure. Acknowledge your desire for change and consider what steps can help bring about this transformation.

Some Questions to Ponder:
- What areas do you sense a "call to adventure" or the need for change and growth?
- What fears or doubts could be stopping you from following this call?
- How can you step outside your comfort zone and begin this journey?

2. Initiation: Trials, Tribulations, and Transformation

The second stage of a Hero's Journey is marked by tests, challenges, and obstacles the hero must conquer. Through these trials, they build strength, learn valuable lessons, and uncover their inner resources - leading to resilience through adversity.

Lesson:

As we navigate difficulties and setbacks in life, we have the chance to build resilience and develop personally. We can create effective coping strategies and problem-solving abilities by accepting and learning from adversity.

Tip:

When faced with obstacles and failures, view them as opportunities for growth rather than insurmountable obstacles. Reflect on past errors and draw upon lessons learned that you can apply to future difficulties.

Example: If you need help with public speaking, join a local Toastmasters club or take a course to hone your skills. Take on the challenge, practice regularly, and receive feedback to become more assured in front of an audience.

Some Questions to Consider:
- What challenges or obstacles have you encountered, or anticipate facing, on your journey?
- What skills, resources, or support systems can you use to overcome these difficulties?
- What lessons have you learned from these experiences - or hope to learn from them in the future?

3. Locating Mentors and Allies

Along the way, heroes may encounter mentors, allies, and enemies who can either aid or hinder their progress.

Lesson:

By seeking support from mentors and allies, we can overcome obstacles and acquire the wisdom to navigate future difficulties. Even those who appear against us (competitors or bad actors, for instance) intentionally or not create opportunities for us to grow through our struggles. After all, a hero without an enemy would make for a rather dull story!

Tip:

Create a support network by surrounding yourself with encouraging individuals who can guide and motivate you. This could include friends, family members, professional mentors, or coaches - even role models you don't directly interact with but who still offer value here, such as authors, entrepreneurs, or other public figures.

Examples:

If you're considering a change of career path, reach out to mentors who have succeeded in your desired field. Attend networking events, join online forums, and ask for introductions to expand your circle of allies.

When faced with competition, please take note of any weaknesses it reveals and create a strategy to strengthen those areas.

Some questions to consider:
- Who in your life can serve as a mentor or ally in encouraging personal growth and resilience?
- What qualities do these individuals possess that make them valuable to your journey?
- How can you seek additional mentors and allies to expand your support system?
- Who are your challengers (competitors, bad actors, etc.), and what lessons can you learn from that adversity?

4. Return: Sharing and Reintegrating Wisdom

In the final stage of a Hero's Journey, the hero returns home transformed by their experiences. They bring back newfound wisdom, skills, or strengths which can benefit themselves and others. However, this stage often involves reintegration as they must learn to apply this newfound insight in real-life settings.

Lesson:

After conquering challenges and developing personally, giving back and sharing our wisdom with others is essential. By doing so, we can inspire and support those just starting on their Hero's Journey. We continue developing resilience and cultivating growth by applying these lessons to everyday living.

Tip:

As you grow and develop resilience, share your experiences with those facing similar struggles. Offer support and motivation, and use your story to motivate others.

Example: If you've successfully navigated a career change, share your journey on social media, write a blog post, or speak at an event near you. Your story may provide hope and inspiration to others considering similar paths while providing learning opportunities.

Some Questions to Ponder:
- What wisdom or insights have you gained from your journey thus far?
- How can you share this understanding to encourage and motivate personal growth and resilience?
- How can you incorporate your newfound understanding and experiences into daily life to continue on your personal development journey?

Your Hero's Journey

The Hero's Journey offers a powerful framework for understanding resilience and personal growth. By accepting change, learning from experience, and giving back to those in need, we can embark on our transformational journey and build the resilience needed to thrive in today's world.

Part 3

Wellness

CHAPTER NINE
Self-Care and Well-Being

Self-care has become a trend lately, and an entire industry has arisen to capitalize on it. On the one hand, self-care offers us many effective practices we may not otherwise discover. Unfortunately, however, many of these more trendy and marketable practices become exclusive to specific demographics and less accessible to everyone who could use them most.

Self-care is more than a luxury. It should be accessible to everyone. Sometimes I come across self-care-style videos of people bathed in soft light, mindfully making artisan tea in a handcrafted mug, and then strolling out into fields of flowers or another idyllic spot. Everything seems perfect - just perfect. Meanwhile, here I am, living an ordinary life, wishing for all those things as if they hold the secret to what I need... as if having that fancy mug, handcrafted tea, or field of flowers will make me feel complete. Why can't I feel complete on my couch with mundane tea and a chipped mug? Treating self-care like a commodity distances us from proper self-care and creates an unattainable illusion - like seeking gold at the end of a rainbow.

In this chapter, we will endeavor to reclaim self-care as something accessible for everyone. However, this comes at the cost of letting go of some of the misconceptions we have been sold.

Defining Self-Care

Self-care is often mistaken for mental health, though the two concepts should be distinct. Taking time off work to relax and de-stress may be called a "mental health day," although self-care and mental health are not synonymous. It encompasses all areas of our life. For example, physical well-being also needs attention through proper sleep, diet, and exercise, applying first aid when hurt or feeling unwell, or getting regular checkups to identify problems early on.

All the physical health items listed are forms of self-care, which makes sense when we consider how intertwined mental, emotional, and physical well-being are. Studies have demonstrated how physical exercise improves mental well-being while anxiety or stress may lead to physical illness - so this concept of "self-care" needs to be taken more literally.

Self-Care is the conscious decision to take responsibility for our overall well-being. That includes mental, emotional, and physical wellness; some might even add spiritual well-being, but since that can be a loaded term, I will leave that option up to those with whom it resonates.

How we take responsibility for our health comes in two forms: Proactive and Reactive.

Proactive Self-Care is all about building resilience to life's inevitable obstacles. It asks how to create a life I don't need to run away from. How can I build more resilience? Some examples include:

- Enhancing overall happiness to help us be more resilient when faced with stress or disappointments.
- Mindfulness training to cultivate awareness of our internal experiences.
- Eating well and getting enough physical activity daily to keep our body and mind healthy and improving how we handle stress.
- Cultivating meaningful relationships to provide us with a support network that will be there when we need it most.
- Saving for unexpected financial struggles learning budget effectively to reduce financial risk.
- Aligning one's actions with one's needs, values, and strengths provides the purpose and meaning to our actions.
- Honing critical thinking skills to see past our biases and the manipulation of others.
- Regularly engaging in "self-care" practices to build resilience

and dedicate intentional time for our well-being (sports, hiking, visiting friends/family, meditation, game nights, spa visits - the list is endless and explicitly tailored to each individual).

- Striving for work-life balance to have time for oneself and create healthy boundaries with work.

Reactive Self-Care is how we respond to active threats to our well-being to lessen their effect. This draws upon the resilience we have built up over time so that those skills can be drawn upon during times of crisis. Reactive Self-Care asks the question: how can I consciously respond in a way which supports my well-being? This may include:

- Acknowledging we have control over how we react.
- Requesting help from friends, family, and professionals as needed.
- Utilizing critical thinking and mindfulness skills to gain more objectivity about the current threat so one can respond based on what occurs rather than what one may perceive it to be.
- Cutting out toxic influences in one's life (fake friends, toxic jobs and relationships, unsafe environments) as they are identified.
- Facing fears and challenges requires taking action rather than choosing to be the victim; sometimes, self-care means getting one's hands dirty doing some unpleasant work.
- Utilize targeted self-care practices when feeling stressed or overwhelmed. Breathing exercises may be beneficial if approached as tools that aid the process rather than an end in themselves.
- Acknowledging disappointment and failure, learning from mistakes, adapting as necessary, and moving forward.

While a trip to the spa may sound appealing, we're investing in a life where we no longer require "mental health days" when our well-being is most fragile.

Self-care is essential for overall well-being and leading a balanced, rewarding life. It consists of our intentional actions to nurture our physical, emotional, and mental well-being. Let's explore some strategies for creating an effective self-care routine.

Physical Self-Care

Physical self-care is about taking good care of one's body by exercising regularly, eating a balanced diet, and sleeping enough. Doing this can improve energy levels, immune system function, and resilience to stress. Furthermore, it helps prevent various health issues, improves mental well-being, and aids emotional regulation. Caring for one's physical needs ultimately sets an empowering foundation for personal growth, productivity, and resilience.

Here are some tips to help you prioritize physical self-care:

1. Get enough sleep: Aim for 7-9 hours per night, experimenting to find the right amount of sleep for your needs. Create a bedtime routine, stick with an established sleep schedule, and create a relaxing sleeping environment.
2. Eat a Balanced Diet: Include various fruits, vegetables, whole grains, lean proteins, and healthy fats in your meals. Moderation and mindful eating can help you achieve this balanced intake. Reducing sugar and processed foods can make a surprising difference in mental clarity and physical health.
3. Exercise Regularly: Aim for at least 150 minutes of moderate-intensity aerobic activity for 75 minutes of vigorous aerobic activity each week. Choose activities you enjoy doing, such as walking, swimming, dancing, or yoga, that you find enjoyable.
4. Stay Hydrated: Drink plenty of water throughout the day to support overall health, digestion, and cognitive function.
5. Schedule Regular Check-Ups: Make sure you visit your healthcare provider for routine check-ups and screenings to stay proactive about your well-being.

Emotional Self-Care

Emotional self-care is essential because it promotes mental well-being and personal growth. By effectively managing emotions, individuals can reduce stress, anxiety, and burnout - ultimately improving their quality of life. Emotional self-care also leads to better decision-making, healthier relationships, and increased resilience during trying times. Prioritizing emotional well-being contributes to a balanced life that provides the basis for personal and professional success.

Here are some strategies to help you prioritize emotional self-care:

1. Express Your Emotions: Reach out to a trusted friend, family member, or therapist and express your emotions. Alternatively, try journaling or creative outlets like painting or music to express yourself emotionally.
2. Practice Mindfulness: Use meditation, deep breathing exercises, or yoga to increase self-awareness and cultivate inner peace.
3. Set Boundaries: Master the art of saying no and creating healthy boundaries in your personal and professional life to protect your emotional well-being.
4. Cultivate a Support System: Create meaningful connections with friends, family, and mentors who offer emotional support, motivation, and understanding.
5. Engage in Hobbies: Do activities that bring you joy and help you relax, such as reading, gardening, or playing an instrument. Find ways to focus on what is important to you.

Mental Self-Care

Mental self-care is paramount as it directly affects psychological well-being, cognitive function, and quality of life. By prioritizing mental health, individuals can cultivate emotional stability, manage stress effectively and keep a balanced perspective. Engaging in mental self-care practices such as mindfulness or relaxation promotes clarity, focus, and creativity, ultimately supporting personal growth, resilience, and the capacity to cope with challenges across personal and professional domains.

Here are some tips to help prioritize mental self-care:

1. Prioritize relaxation: Set aside time each day to unwind and relax, whether through taking a bath, reading a book, or engaging in meditation.
2. Limit screen time: Create boundaries around screen time, especially before bedtime, to protect your mental health and promote restorative sleep.
3. Learn something new: Stretch yourself intellectually by learning a new language, skill, or hobby.
4. Practice Gratitude: Foster a spirit of gratitude by keeping a

gratitude journal or showing others your appreciation.

5. Seek Professional Help: For support and advice, speak with a mental health professional such as a therapist or counselor if you are experiencing mental health difficulties.

Constructing Your Customized Self-Care Routine

When creating a comprehensive self-care regimen, incorporate elements from each abovementioned category. Begin by assessing your current habits and pinpointing areas for improvement. Be realistic about the time and resources you can dedicate to self-care activities; even small changes can make a big difference.

Consistency of practice encourages the formation of healthy habits, making it easier to sustain self-care practices and reap their ongoing rewards. It also builds resiliency to help one get through times of hardship. While one-off self-care exercises may provide temporary comfort or reduce stress, consistent practice cultivates skills and resiliency, which will reap long-term rewards.

Finally, it's important to remember that self-care is not a one-size-fits-all solution. Paying attention to your body and mind is essential to adjust your routine as necessary. Investing in yourself and prioritizing self-care will promote a healthier, happier, and more balanced life.

Here are some steps to help you create a personalized self-care routine:

1. Assess Your Needs: Take stock of your physical, emotional, and mental requirements. Identify areas where you feel depleted or overwhelmed and consider how self-care can address those concerns.

2. Create Realistic Goals: Set specific, achievable objectives for each area of self-care. Be mindful of your schedule and other commitments, and remember that small, consistent actions are more beneficial than one-off, unsustainable gestures.

3. Plan Your Routine: Create a daily, weekly, or monthly self-care schedule incorporating your desired activities. Prioritize the essential self-care practices and make them part of your regular regimen.

4. Track Your Progress: Monitor your self-care activities and evaluate their effects on your well-being. Adjust your routine

as necessary to guarantee it remains efficient and sustainable.

5. Be Flexible and Forgiving: Recognize that life's demands sometimes interfere with your self-care routine. Be open to adapting your plan as necessary, and be kind to yourself if you miss a self-care activity or goal.

6. Find Support: Communicate your self-care goals and routine with friends, family, or a support group. They can offer encouragement, motivation, and accountability. Finding others who share similar interests is beneficial, too; for instance, joining in on morning group jogs adds to the sense of camaraderie while encouraging you not to skip out on mornings when weather conditions are less than ideal.

7. Re-evaluate Regularly: Review your self-care routine to ensure it still meets your needs and supports your overall well-being. Pay attention to how these activities affect your moods, energy levels, and general well-being; this awareness can help you fine-tune your routine as necessary and adjust as circumstances or priorities change. Remember that self-care is a dynamic process requiring flexibility and compassion toward yourself.

By creating a personalized self-care routine that incorporates physical, emotional, and mental practices for self-care, you will be better equipped to tackle life's difficulties, promote resilience and achieve balance in your life. Remember: self-care is an ongoing journey that changes according to your needs and circumstances.

The Importance of Mental Health

A discussion on Self-care would not be complete without acknowledging and addressing mental health needs. The pandemic has brought about many changes to our lives, such as remote work, increased technological dependence, social isolation, and economic instability; additionally, AI's rapid advancement has added further uncertainty to many professions. All of these have profoundly affected our mental well-being, making it even more crucial than ever to understand and meet those needs.

This section will address the most prevalent mental health

concerns during these trying times: anxiety, depression, and isolation. We'll assess their importance to our well-being and offer practical strategies for addressing these worries.

Recognizing and Addressing Anxiety and Depression

The pandemic has taken a toll on mental health worldwide, leading many people to experience increased anxiety and depression. Recognizing the signs of these conditions is the first step toward getting help; common symptoms include persistent sadness or hopelessness, excessive worry, changes in sleep or appetite, and loss of interest in activities you once enjoyed. If any of these symptoms apply to you or someone close to you, consider seeking professional assistance when it impacts one's quality of life.

As we will discuss further in the chapter on Rediscovering Human Connection, depression and anxiety can manifest differently for different people. This means individuals may experience different degrees of severity and the manifestation of these mental health conditions. Both disorders present with a spectrum of symptoms and levels of intensity, from mild to severe, depending on factors like genetics, environmental influences, and personal experiences. Unfortunately, this book - or any presentation - cannot diagnose or treat you for these issues. However, I hope this guide can educate you so you can better recognize when something's amiss and find the support you require. In this section, we'll examine anxiety and depression's role in mental health and ways of recognizing and treating these conditions with compassion.

Anxiety vs. Depression

Anxiety is a normal stress response and can take various forms, such as constant worry, restlessness, irritability, or difficulty concentrating. While some anxiety is normal, excessive amounts can disrupt daily life and negatively affect well-being. Depression, on the other hand, manifests itself by persistent sadness or loss of interest in activities once enjoyed; this leads to emotional and physical symptoms like fatigue, sleep disturbances, irritability, and feelings of worthlessness or hopelessness.

Recognizing anxiety and depression requires paying close attention to your thoughts, emotions, and behaviors.

Some common signs of anxiety include:

1. Excessive worry or fear
2. Rapid heartbeat or breathing
3. Difficulty concentrating or making decisions
4. Irritability or mood swings
5. Sleep disturbances, such as insomnia or restless sleep

For depression, look for symptoms such as:

1. Persistent sadness, hopelessness, or emptiness
2. Loss of interest or pleasure in activities you once enjoyed
3. Changes in appetite or weight
4. Fatigue or low energy
5. Feelings of guilt or worthlessness

If you believe someone close to you is struggling with anxiety or depression, they must receive professional assistance from a mental health professional. They can accurately diagnose the problem and suggest appropriate treatments.

In addition to seeking professional help, there are several supplemental self-help strategies you can employ to address anxiety and depression:

1. Practice self-compassion: Be kind and understanding when facing difficult times; treat yourself with empathy and gentleness.
2. Engage in regular physical activity: Research has demonstrated that exercise can help alleviate anxiety and depression by releasing "feel-good" chemicals called endorphins.
3. Cultivate a Support Network: Connect with friends, family, or support groups to share your experiences and feelings. Social connections can help alleviate feelings of isolation and offer invaluable emotional assistance.
4. Establish a Daily Routine: An organized schedule can give one the feeling of structure and control during uncertain times. For instance, keep to one's sleep schedule and personal grooming routines (showers, changing out of sleepwear, brushing teeth), etc.
5. Practice Relaxation Techniques: Deep breathing exercises,

progressive muscle relaxation, and mindfulness meditation can help reduce anxiety and elevate moods.

6. Educate Yourself: Read books and watch videos that discuss your condition; However, these alone won't cure it; understanding what's going on and how others have overcome it can be a great help in feeling less overwhelmed and helpless.

Isolation

Social isolation and loneliness have become all too common during the pandemic due to necessary precautions taken to slow its spread. As we spend more time indoors and limit physical contact with others, our social interactions become less frequent and less fulfilling. Even with lessening restrictions, remote work may keep us physically distant from friends and family, decreasing opportunities for face-to-face mingling. This lack of connection may cause loneliness even for those who hadn't felt them before the crisis started.

Tips and Strategies to Combat Isolation:

1. Maintain Regular Communication with Friends and Family: Make time each day or week to call, text, or video chat with loved ones. Regular contact helps maintain social connections while decreasing feelings of isolation.

2. Participate in (or start) virtual events: Many organizations have responded to the pandemic by hosting online workshops, webinars, and social gatherings. For instance, join a virtual book club to discuss your favorite books with other bookworms!

3. Cultivate Hobbies and Interests: Pursuing personal interests can provide a sense of accomplishment and help combat feelings of isolation. Engaging in activities that bring joy also presents chances to connect with others who share similar passions.

4. Maintain Physical Exercise: Exercise has long been known to benefit mental health. Regular physical activity can reduce stress, anxiety, and feelings of isolation. Participating in group exercise classes - even virtual ones - fosters community and connection.

5. Talk About It: In our society, many of us tend to avoid showing vulnerability regarding mental health concerns. Reach out to those closest to you and share how you feel. There are also online support groups and mental health professionals who can offer additional help in person and via phone or video conferencing.

6. Get out! The pandemic is (mostly?) over, and restrictions have been eased. If you are still uncomfortable without your mask, keep it on but get outside. Reach out to friends and family to reconnect - these meetings can occur outdoors if people still desire some social distancing. Picnics, hikes, window shopping excursions - plenty of low-risk activities would allow in-person reconnection.

Feeling isolated can lead us to believe we are more isolated from the world than we are. It can be easy to slip into a despairing mood, so breaking out of that bubble is essential for well-being. Even small steps can significantly affect one's quality of life.

Seeking Professional Help

This has become a theme in this book, but with good reason. It is vital to seek professional assistance when necessary. My struggles with depression over a decade ago and the struggles I have witnessed in others close to me have taught me the critical importance of seeking help when overwhelmed. Depression and anxiety will lie to you, giving you a sense that there are no options available for improving the situation, and they are very, very effective with those lies. Finding help is your best defense against these demons. In those moments when you feel most helpless and hopeless, help is most needed, and it can be heartbreaking to realize how many have missed chances of healing because they did not reach out for help. I have lost people close to me due to this, and I would not wish that on you or your loved ones.

If you're struggling with your mental health, it is essential to seek professional assistance. A therapist or counselor can offer invaluable insight and support, helping you better comprehend your feelings and develop successful coping methods.

Reaching out for help is not a sign of weakness - it is a sign of strength and courage.

The Value of Professional Help

Since I seem to have become list-happy while writing this book, let me briefly highlight some of the key reasons why seeking professional help is so beneficial:

1. Expert Advice: Mental health professionals have years of education, training, and expertise. They can offer evidence-based strategies and techniques to help you manage your emotions, thoughts, and behaviors.

2. Objective Perspective: When struggling with mental health, gaining perspective or reasoning rationally can be difficult. A mental health professional can offer an objective viewpoint, helping identify patterns or areas of concern you may not have noticed.

3. Personalized Support: Professional assistance is tailored to meet your needs and circumstances. Mental health professionals can work with you on developing coping strategies and interventions specific to your situation and individual struggles.

4. Safe Space for Self-Expression: Therapy or counseling sessions provide a confidential, nonjudgmental space where you can openly express your thoughts, feelings, and experiences without fear of judgment or criticism.

5. Trained/Educated Responses: While having friends and family to talk to can be helpful, they may not know how to support you in times of difficulty effectively. How many depressed people have been told "cheer up" or "look on the bright side" with good intentions? While these individuals mean well, they lack professional training on how to respond like a professional would.

6. Early Intervention: Seeking professional assistance early on can prevent minor problems from becoming more prominent. Early intervention provides healthy coping strategies and helps address underlying issues before they become overwhelming.

7. Improved Overall Well-Being: Professional help addresses specific mental health issues and can contribute to overall

well-being. Therapy may improve relationships, communication skills, self-esteem, and life satisfaction.

8. Medication Management (when necessary): Medication may be prescribed as part of a comprehensive treatment plan. Psychiatrists and other mental health professionals can assist in managing medications, monitoring their effectiveness, and adjusting dosages as necessary.

Getting the Most Out of Professional Help

To maximize the advantages of professional help, it's essential to:

1. Be open and honest: Express your thoughts, feelings, and experiences with a mental health professional so they can better comprehend your situation and offer supportive solutions.

2. Actively Participate: Take an active role in the process, ask questions, and be willing to try new strategies and techniques.

3. Be Patient: Mental health improvement takes time and dedication - be patient with yourself and the process; change may not occur immediately, and your therapist needs time to understand your situation.

4. Communicate Your Needs: If a particular approach or technique isn't working, speak up and share your worries with a mental health professional. They want to provide you with a session that works for your needs.

CHAPTER TEN
Cultivating Gratitude and Positivity

I have referenced the benefits of gratitude a few times throughout this book, and this chapter is dedicated to exploring it in more detail. The chapter is a bit smaller than the others because I wanted to focus specifically on this topic since it plays a more critical role in one's well-being than is often given credit. Initially, this was part of the general Self-Care chapter, but I was concerned it would get lost among the other topics.

Research has shown that regularly practicing gratitude can help to reduce stress, improve sleep, boost mood, increase resilience, and enhance social connections. Regarding one's well-being, cultivating appreciation and positivity is an excellent addition to one's self-care routine. By focusing on the positive aspects of our lives and expressing gratitude for what we have, we can create a more optimistic outlook and experience greater happiness.

I have to be honest here. For years I scoffed at the idea of "practicing gratitude," such as maintaining a gratitude journal. It had a certain new-age fluffy vibe that sounded nice but lacked substance. At one point, a friend began to post what she was grateful for daily on Facebook. After *two years*, her posts for gratefulness were long and detailed. I decided to try it out in my private journal. As expected, it was initially clunky, and I had to push to find something to write about. After a while, I began to see many little things I was grateful for - the sound my heating system makes when the heat kicks in, the snore of my cat, a pink sunrise in winter, the way the guy at the local corner breakfast cart remembers how I like my tea - and sure enough, I felt better. We are surrounded by small moments of joy, beauty, and kindness, but they are often drowned out by the hustle and bustle of modern life and our ruminations. As I began to research ways to bring more joy into my life, the notes of which I am using to write this chapter, I found plenty of studies showing the benefits a regular gratitude practice has on one's well-being. So this was a big lesson for me not to cling to my assumptions blindly!

Practicing Gratitude

The actual practice of gratitude is relatively straightforward... in theory. It is the act of intentionally recognizing and appreciating the positive things in our lives, big and small. It gives us a moment to focus on the positive in our lives and express appreciation for them through thoughts, words, art, or actions.

Below we'll explore a few practical ways to practice and increase gratitude and positivity in one's life. While the practice is easy, it can take time before it feels natural, so be patient with yourself. As with any skill, consistency, of course, pays off over time.

Keep a Gratitude Journal

Set aside a few minutes each day to reflect on and write down three to five things you're grateful for, whether small or insignificant. It can be associated with ordinary events, personal attributes, or valued people in your life... whatever feels right. Example: Today, I am grateful for the beautiful sunrise, the delicious breakfast my partner made, and the opportunity to learn something new at work. Whether you elaborate on these items or list them is up to you. The important thing is to come up with a list.

A related journaling practice that focuses on positivity is to write down uplifting or inspirational quotes and clippings of artwork and photos that bring you joy.

Gratitude Journal Prompts

Gratitude journal prompts are questions or statements designed to encourage reflection and focus on the positive aspects of life. The prompts below help when you are having problems thinking of ideas and offer an opportunity to think outside of your usual thought patterns. Consider randomly choosing two or three prompts when writing in your journal. If you do not have a journaling practice, this can be a great way to start developing that habit. You can find plenty more prompts online and in the companion workbook.

1. List three things you are grateful for today and explain why.
2. Describe a person in your life for whom you are deeply grateful. Elaborate on why you hold that gratitude.
3. Write about a challenging experience that ultimately led to personal growth and express your gratitude.
4. List five things you love about your home and explain why they make you grateful.
5. Recall a time when someone showed you kindness. How did it make you feel, and why are you grateful for that moment?
6. Describe a place that brings you peace and gratitude.
7. Write about a moment when you felt deeply grateful for your health or body.
8. List three things you appreciate about your work or career.
9. Reflect on a lesson you learned from a mistake or failure and why you are grateful for the experience.
10. Describe a happy childhood memory and explain why it brings you gratitude.
11. Write about a book, movie, or song that has positively impacted your mood and express gratitude.
12. List five small, everyday things that bring you joy and gratitude.
13. Describe an act of generosity you've witnessed or experienced, and explain why it made you feel grateful.
14. Reflect on a time when you overcame a fear or obstacle, and explain why you are grateful for the experience.
15. Write about a favorite hobby or activity that brings you gratitude.
16. List three personal strengths or qualities you're grateful for and explain why.
17. Describe a time when you helped someone and how it made you feel grateful.
18. Write about a particular tradition or celebration that brings you gratitude.

19. Reflect on a time when you practiced self-care and why you're grateful for that moment.
20. Describe a beautiful moment in nature that filled you with gratitude.

Share Your Gratitude with Others

Research has found that expressing gratitude can strengthen relationships and spread positivity. Express your appreciation to the people in your life through verbal or written communication. Say, thank you to people who have done something kind or helpful for you, or let people who bring you joy know you recognize this and appreciate them in your life.

Go Through the Motions

Grateful motions include smiling, saying thank you, and writing letters of gratitude. By "going through the motions of gratitude," you'll trigger the emotion of gratitude more often.

As for using this to spread positivity, performing random acts of kindness benefits both the doer and the recipient. Do something kind for someone else without expecting anything in return. My personal favorite is swiping someone into the subway with my spare metro card when I see they are having problems with their card. Not only is it a random act of kindness for the person whose card had expired, but it speeds the rest of my fellow commuters through the New York rush hour.

Cultivating a Positive Environment

Creating a positive environment can help reinforce one's gratitude and positivity practices. Surround yourself with uplifting and inspiring quotes, images, or artwork, and minimize exposure to negative influences, such as excessive news consumption, toxic relationships, and senseless drama. Engage in activities that bring you joy and help you maintain a positive mindset, such as listening to uplifting music, spending time in nature, or engaging in a creative hobby.

Experience Your Senses

One of the warm-up exercises I do in every forest therapy session I host at Hudson Valley Forest Therapy is to invite participants to close their eyes and scan their environment with their remaining senses — touch, smell, taste, and hearing. My clients will often share how alive it made them feel and how it encouraged a sense of gratitude for their surroundings.

When we savor the world around us through our senses, we can gain a deeper appreciation for the things around us that often go unnoticed and a better appreciation for the ability of our bodies to sense so much variety.

Find the Positive

When faced with a difficulty, consider searching for positive aspects/interpretations of a situation. For example, what did you learn? Try finding three such examples. This may be challenging! Aim to develop a habit of reframing things positively. That does not mean denying the negative aspects of such difficulties, but instead exploring other more positive perspectives for a more holistic viewpoint.

Closing Tips to Support Practicing Gratitude

Below are some tips to support you in your practice:

- Make a Vow to Practice Gratitude: Research has shown that making a public or private oath to perform a behavior increases the likelihood that one will follow through with the action. This phenomenon is known as the "oath effect." Consider writing your gratitude vow, which could be as simple as "I vow to count my blessings each day," Post it somewhere where you will be reminded of it daily.
- Practice mindfulness and presence: Incorporate mindfulness techniques, such as meditation or deep breathing exercises, into your daily routine. Mindfulness can help you become more present and aware of the positive aspects of your life. Example: During a meditation session, focus on the sensation of your breath and the feeling of gratitude for this opportunity to spend quality time with yourself.
- Focus on the small things: Gratitude doesn't have to be reserved for significant events or accomplishments. The little things in life can often bring the most joy and appreciation.

Example: Take a moment to be grateful for the warm sun on your face, the aroma of your morning coffee, or the laughter of a loved one.

- Practice gratitude during challenging times: It's essential to practice gratitude during difficult situations, as it can help shift your perspective and foster resilience. Example: If you're going through a tough time at work, be grateful for the opportunity to learn and grow from the experience.
- Fostering positive relationships: Surrounding yourself with positive, supportive people can significantly influence your outlook on life. Nurture relationships with friends and family members who uplift and inspire you, and seek new connections with like-minded individuals. Offer support and encouragement to others, and be open to receiving it in return.

As you can see, this is a relatively easy practice on the surface. The main challenge is making such a practice a habit and part of your daily routine. While it may feel awkward initially, it will not take long to normalize, at which point it will begin to foster a more positive mindset.

Have fun with this! With all the effort some of these chapters are asking of you, it's nice to be grateful for such a simple yet effective practice. (See what I did there?)

CHAPTER ELEVEN

Social Skills and Social Anxiety

According to a brief published by the World Health Organization (WHO), the global prevalence of depression and anxiety rose by 25% in the first year following the COVID-19 pandemic. This brief highlighted the most affected as being women and young people.

The reason for this increase has to do with multiple stress factors. The pandemic caused unprecedented stress and isolation, factoring as a significant reason for the rise in mental health cases. This was linked to limitations in people's ability and willingness to seek support from their loved ones, work, and get involved in their communities. Fear of infection, loneliness, financial worries, and suffering for oneself or loved ones have all been mentioned as stressors that can lead to anxiety and depression.

As we enter this new stage of recovery from the pandemic, restrictions have largely been lifted or at least reduced. With more employees returning to the office and people, in general, returning to some semblance of social life, the effects of the pandemic are still taking their toll on mental health, so many are finding this transition difficult. Those who may not have experienced social anxiety previously may find themselves experiencing it on some level now. For some, this is a mild awkwardness that will dissipate in time, and for others, it may require the support of a professional, with many falling somewhere in between. This chapter is intended as a starting point to help those in need better understand what they are experiencing and what they can do about it.

Identifying the Stressors

Social anxiety has been significantly magnified for some due to factors related to the pandemic, such as:

1. Social Isolation: Lockdowns, social distancing measures, and remote work have reduced social interactions, leading to feelings of loneliness and the atrophy of our social skillsets. This isolation may have amplified preexisting social anxiety or caused it to flare up for those who weren't previously prone to it.

2. Increased Reliance on Digital Communication: The pandemic has forced many social interactions onto digital platforms such as video calls, online meetings, and social media. For some people, this change may have increased their anxiety levels, making them feel self-conscious about their appearance or struggle with the nuances of digital communication.

3. Fear of Infection: People with social anxiety may worry that they will contract the virus during social encounters, leading them to avoid these situations even as the restrictions ease.

4. Alterations to social skills: Prolonged isolation or limited social contact can erode social abilities, leading to anxiety when people re-engage with other people.

5. Adjustment to new social norms: As the pandemic ushered in new models, such as wearing masks and maintaining physical distance, those with social anxiety may have found adjusting back to pre-pandemic norms more challenging. Additionally, while some of the pandemic-related norms become less relevant or enforced, their inconsistent practice still contributes to uncertainty and fear as people attempt to navigate these expectations. When does one need a mask? How does one shake hands these days - are we still fist-bumping? Is hugging back in play? These are all questions I have wrestled with this week alone!

6. Uncertainty and Stress: The pandemic has created an atmosphere of unease and stress that may exacerbate existing mental health conditions such as social anxiety and depression.

7. Economic and societal stressors: The pandemic has caused widespread job loss, financial insecurity, and uncertainty

about the future. These stresses can contribute to increased anxiety levels - including social anxiety.

8. Re-Entry Anxiety: As restrictions lift and people return to pre-pandemic social activities, some may experience "re-entry anxiety." This anxiety may stem from worries about resuming social interactions, adapting to new routines, or fearing judgment from others about their behavior during the crisis. Furthermore, having become accustomed to remote communication methods like video calls and messaging, returning in person for socializing again may cause anxiety-provoking feelings.

Understanding Social Anxiety

Formal social anxiety is characterized by an intense and persistent fear of social situations, often due to worries about judgment or humiliation. This can lead to embarrassment, self-consciousness, or avoidance of social interactions. Recognizing your social anxiety is the first step toward taking steps toward managing it effectively.

Social anxiety can be divided into two distinct types:

- Specific Social Anxiety (or Performance Social Anxiety): This form of social anxiety is related to particular situations or activities that involve performance or being observed by others. People with specific social anxiety may experience intense fear when faced with public speaking, performing on stage, singing, taking exams, or participating in sports events; however, their fear is usually limited to these circumstances, and they may feel comfortable in other social settings.

- Generalized Social Anxiety: Generalized social anxiety is a more widespread fear and anxiety individuals experience in social situations. People suffering from generalized social anxiety may have trouble initiating conversations, attending gatherings, meeting new people, eating in public, or making phone calls; all these activities can significantly impact daily functioning and quality of life.

Here are some common signs of social anxiety:

1. Fear of public speaking: Individuals suffering from social anxiety may dread giving presentations or speeches or speaking in small groups.

2. Avoidance of Social Events: People suffering from social anxiety may avoid parties, gatherings, and other social settings out of fear of judgment or feel uncomfortable.

3. Difficulty Forming New Relationships: Social anxiety may make meeting new people challenging, and forming friendships or romantic connections can be difficult.

4. Fear of Being Focused on: People with social anxiety might feel intense discomfort when others focus on them, whether during conversation or while engaging in an activity.

5. Anxiety about Eating or Drinking Publicly: People with social anxiety may worry about being judged or scrutinized while eating or drinking in front of others, leading them to avoid restaurants and other public places where they might need to eat.

6. Difficulty with small talk: Individuals suffering from social anxiety may find it challenging to engage in casual conversations with strangers or acquaintances due to the fear of saying something embarrassing or being judged.

7. Fear of using public restrooms: People with social anxiety may feel self-conscious or worried about being judged while using public restrooms, leading to avoidance or significant distress when needing these facilities.

8. Social anxiety may manifest as an excessive worry about being judged or criticized, even when there may be no legitimate cause for concern.

9. Physical Symptoms of Social Anxiety: Physical signs of social anxiety may include blushing, sweating, trembling, rapid heartbeat, or difficulty breathing in social settings.

10. Avoidance of Eye Contact: People suffering from social anxiety may avoid making eye contact during conversations, as they may feel exposed or fear others' judgment.

Remember that experiencing nervousness or discomfort in social settings is common, and the tips in this chapter will be especially suitable for you. However, if the anxiety becomes excessive, persistent, and significantly impacts daily life, this could indicate a social anxiety disorder. In such cases, seeking help from a mental health professional is recommended to develop effective coping strategies and receive appropriate treatment. I cannot emphasize the importance of seeking professional assistance when dealing with something difficult.

For those experiencing mild discomfort, a few strategies may help manage symptoms and enhance overall well-being. But please keep in mind: I am an advocate for mental healthcare, not a healthcare provider - so this (or any other book) should never replace professional assistance when needed.

Developing (Healthy) Coping Mechanisms

Coping mechanisms are an invaluable tool in managing social anxiety in challenging circumstances. Try deep breathing exercises, grounding techniques, or mindfulness meditation to relax the mind and body. Journaling your efforts and tracking progress in a journal can also be immensely helpful here.

Here are some strategies you can use to manage social anxiety and develop healthy coping mechanisms effectively:

1. Be Aware of Your Triggers: Begin by identifying situations that cause you anxiety. These could include specific social interactions or events. By understanding your triggers, you can better prepare yourself and create strategies to manage them when they arise. (And not simply avoid the triggers.)

2. Practice Deep Breathing and Relaxation Techniques: Deep breathing, mindfulness meditation, and progressive muscle relaxation can help to relax your mind and reduce anxiety. Practice these techniques regularly to be prepared to use them effectively in anxiety-provoking situations.

3. Challenge Negative Thoughts: Social anxiety often stems from irrational fears and negative thinking patterns. Recognize these thoughts, question their validity, and replace them with more realistic and positive ones.

4. Gradual Exposure: Gradually expose yourself to anxiety-provoking situations in a controlled way, starting with favorable conditions and working up to more challenging ones. This will help you build confidence and desensitize yourself to anxiety triggers.

5. Develop Assertiveness and Communication Skills: Gain the ability to express yourself honestly without being aggressive

or passive. Effective communication will boost your self-assurance in social settings and reduce anxiety levels.

6. Prepare and Practice: If you're anxious about an event or situation, prepare for it. Practice saying what you plan on saying, using your body language, and visualize yourself succeeding in the scenario. Doing this can help reduce anxiety levels and boost confidence levels in the situation.

7. Seek Support: Contact trusted friends or family members who offer comfort and understanding. They may also assist in honing social skills and providing a safe space to share experiences.

8. Adopt a Healthy Lifestyle: Exercising regularly, consuming nutritious food, and getting enough sleep each night can improve your mental and physical well-being, making it easier to cope with anxiety.

9. Expand Your Comfort Zone: Push yourself to try new social situations or activities, even if you initially feel uncomfortable. Over time, as your fears subside and you gain experience, your anxiety may decrease and your confidence increase.

10. Educate Yourself: Gain awareness of social anxiety and how it impacts your behavior in social settings. Please recognize that this is a widespread issue many people face, but techniques and strategies are available to manage it effectively.

Consider Seeking Professional Help

If your social anxiety severely interferes with your life or shows no signs of improvement, consider seeking professional assistance from a therapist or counselor. Cognitive-behavioral therapy (CBT) and exposure therapy have been known to be successful treatments for social anxiety. Self-help books can only go so far in what they can offer.

Substituting Self-Criticism with Self-Compassion

Instead of condemning yourself for your anxiety or perceived shortcomings, practice kindness and understanding toward yourself.

Everyone experiences stress and fear at some point, and it's normal to feel nervous in social settings. By showing kindness towards yourself, you can create an internal environment that reduces social anxiety's triggers and effects. Even in cases where your anxiety is severe, you owe it to yourself to get the help you need and move forward with your recovery.

We previously explored self-compassion in more depth in our section on building resilience, so here are some of its benefits when dealing with social anxiety:

1. Reducing Self-Criticicism: Social anxiety often involves harsh self-judgment and negative self-talk. But practicing self-compassion allows you to acknowledge that everyone has setbacks and experiences stress at times - helping counteract self-criticism and giving a more balanced perspective on your experiences.

2. Reducing Isolation: Social anxiety can often lead to feelings of loneliness and isolation. Exercise self-compassion to remember everyone experiences difficulties, so you're not alone in your struggle with social anxiety. Explore ways to counter that sense of isolation.

3. Creating a supportive inner dialogue: Fostering self-compassion helps replace negative self-talk with more understanding and supportive words, which can immensely affect your mindset and ability to manage social anxiety effectively.

Building Social Skills

Improving one's social skills can boost confidence and help reduce social anxiety. Like any skill, social skills must be actively practiced, or they can atrophy. Even many extroverts found the emergence from the COVID-19 lockdowns challenging, feeling rusty in their social skills.

Building social skills to improve communication and connection involves practicing various aspects of interpersonal interaction. Start by practicing small, achievable goals, such as initiating conversations or attending social events with a trusted friend. Gradually increase the complexity and frequency of your social interactions, and celebrate your successes. Remember, social skills are like any other; they can be developed and improved with practice.

Here are some tips to help you develop these skills:

1. Active listening: Pay attention to what others are saying, show that you're engaged by maintaining eye contact, nodding, and using verbal acknowledgments such as "uh-huh" or "I see." Avoid interrupting and try to understand the speaker's point of view.

2. Develop empathy: Work on understanding and sharing the feelings of others. Practice putting yourself in their shoes to understand their perspectives and emotions better. (We will discuss this in more detail later in this section.)

3. Improve nonverbal communication: Pay attention to body language, facial expressions, and tone of voice. Learn to read these cues, respond appropriately, and be aware of your nonverbal signals.

4. Ask open-ended questions: Encourage conversation by asking questions that require more than a simple "yes" or "no" answer. This helps engage others in meaningful conversations and shows your interest in their thoughts and experiences.

5. Practice effective communication: Be clear and concise in your speech. Adjust your communication style depending on your audience and the conversation context. Consider using storytelling to make your messages more engaging and relatable.

6. Be approachable and friendly: Smile, maintain eye contact, and use a warm tone of voice. Show genuine interest in others and be open to meeting new people.

7. Learn to manage conflict: Develop skills to handle disagreements and conflicts constructively. Focus on finding common ground, understanding different perspectives, and working toward a mutually acceptable resolution.

8. Build emotional intelligence: Work on understanding and managing your emotions, as well as recognizing and responding to the feelings of others. Emotional intelligence is crucial for effective communication and building solid connections.

9. Practice assertiveness: Learn to express your thoughts, feelings, and needs respectfully and confidently while respecting the rights and opinions of others.

10. Engage in active socializing: Join clubs and groups, or attend events to meet new people and practice social skills in different settings. The more you practice, the more comfortable and skilled you will become in social situations.

11. Seek feedback: Ask for feedback from friends, family, or mentors on improving your social skills. This can help you identify areas for growth and develop strategies for improvement.

12. Self-reflection: Regularly reflect on your social interactions and identify areas to improve. This will help you become more self-aware and intentional in your communication and connections. Note there is a difference between self-reflection and rumination. If you had an awkward encounter and are ruminating on the negative experience, explore what you can learn from it and move forward, ready to do better next time, even if in baby steps.

13. Observe and learn: Watch others who seem comfortable and confident in social situations. Pay attention to their body language, tone of voice, and conversational style. Use their techniques as inspiration to develop your social skills.

14. Role-play: Practice conversations with someone you trust, such as a close friend or family member, a mentor, or even a professional coach or therapist. This will help you gain confidence in navigating social situations and give you a chance to receive constructive feedback.

Be patient and persistent here. Developing social skills takes time and practice, just like any other skill. For some, it is more accessible than others, but we all can improve. Keep pushing yourself to engage in social situations; your confidence and skills will grow over time.

Developing Empathy and Compassion

Empathy and compassion are fundamental for creating a sense of community and belonging. While I have had a tendency to lump these words together throughout this book, empathy and compassion are two distinct concepts. Empathy involves understanding another person's emotions, while compassion goes further by showing deep concern for their well-being - especially when someone suffers. Compassion combines empathetic understanding with the drive to act and provide assistance, emphasizing emotional connection and the desire to help.

By seeking to understand the experiences and emotions of others, we can build strong, supportive relationships that promote our well-being and resilience and create an inclusive atmosphere where everyone can thrive. As we grapple with the difficulties caused by the pandemic, these traits can help us better comprehend and support one another, thus strengthening our connections and creating more inclusive, resilient communities.

Let's explore each of these concepts in more detail.

Empathy

Empathy is the capacity for someone to understand and share another person's emotions or feelings. It involves placing oneself in their shoes and connecting with their emotional experiences. To cultivate empathy, be curious about others' experiences, practice perspective-taking, and reflect on your emotions and reactions.

Here are some ways to enhance your empathetic skills:

1. Active listening: Pay close attention to what others say verbally and non-verbally without interrupting or jumping to conclusions. Show that you are genuinely interested in their thoughts and emotions. (We will explore more about this later in the chapter.)

2. Be present: Give your full attention to the person you're interacting with, whether in person or virtually. Being present demonstrates that you value and respect their thoughts and feelings. Note how often your mind is on developing your responses rather than listening and bring your focus back to the speaker.

3. Validate emotions: Acknowledge and validate the feelings of others, even if you don't necessarily agree with their perspective. This shows that you respect their feelings and are trying to understand their experience.

4. Embrace curiosity: Approach conversations with an open mind and a genuine desire to learn about the other person's experiences, thoughts, and emotions. Ask questions to understand better where the person is coming from.

5. Engage in perspective-taking: Try to see situations from the other person's viewpoint. This exercise can help you appreciate their emotions and experiences more fully.

6. Cultivate self-awareness: Reflect on your own emotions and reactions, and recognize how they might influence your interactions with others. By understanding yourself, you'll be better equipped to empathize with others.

7. Suspend judgment: Set aside your own opinions, beliefs, and assumptions while listening to the other person. This helps create a safe space to share their feelings and experiences.

8. Show empathy in your responses: Use empathetic language and phrases, such as "That sounds difficult" or "I can understand why you would feel that way," to convey your understanding and support. (Btu only when you mean it - authenticity is important here!)

9. Observe non-verbal cues: Pay attention to body language, facial expressions, and tone of voice to gain insight into the emotions and feelings of others.

10. Learn from diverse experiences: Expand your understanding of different cultures, backgrounds, and life experiences by engaging in conversations, reading books, watching films, and attending events that expose you to various perspectives.

By practicing these techniques, you can develop your empathy skills and become more in tune with the emotions and experiences of those around you.

Compassion

Compassion goes beyond simply understanding and sharing emotions. It engenders intense concern and care for the well-being of others - especially when they are suffering or in need. Compassion inspires individuals to act and offer assistance or support to reduce suffering for those affected. Ultimately, compassion is characterized by empathy and a desire to assist.

To be more compassionate, consider incorporating the following

practices into your daily life:
1. Cultivate empathy: Strive to understand and share the feelings of others by actively listening, being present, and imagining yourself in their shoes.
2. Practice non-judgment: As with developing empathy, refrain from judging others and approach them with an open mind and a willingness to understand their perspectives and experiences. From the standpoint of compassion, how can you actively create a safe space without judgment?
3. Offer support and encouragement: Reach out to others facing challenges, providing a listening ear, a helping hand, or a kind word. By demonstrating compassion, you can create a stronger sense of connection.
4. Be kind: Perform acts of kindness, both big and small, to uplift and support those around you.
5. Practice self-compassion: Treat yourself with the same kindness, understanding, and care you would offer others. Recognize your struggles and give yourself permission to be imperfect.
6. Develop patience: Exercise patience and tolerance when interacting with others, recognizing that everyone has challenges and personal growth journeys.
7. Volunteer: Engage in volunteer work or community service to help those in need and contribute to the well-being of others.
8. Express gratitude: Practice gratitude regularly, acknowledging the positive aspects of your life and the contributions of others.
9. Be present: Stay present in your interactions, giving them your full attention and demonstrating genuine interest in their thoughts and feelings.
10. Educate yourself: Learn about the experiences and struggles of others, especially those from different backgrounds, to foster a deeper understanding and empathy.

The Value of Empathy and Compassion

As fundamental aspects of developing social skills, empathy and compassion promote emotional intelligence, effective communication, and building and maintaining positive relationships. By fostering these qualities, individuals can improve their interpersonal relationships and navigate social situations more effectively.

Here's why empathy and compassion are vital for re-establishing and maintaining human connections:

1. Enhances communication: Empathy and compassion allow us to understand others' perspectives and emotions better, enabling us to communicate more effectively. By putting ourselves in someone else's shoes, we can address their concerns, provide support, and create a stronger connection.

2. Deepens relationships: Empathy and compassion can facilitate more profound, meaningful connections by creating a sense of understanding and validation. Demonstrating that we genuinely care about another person's feelings and experiences helps build trust and strengthen our bond.

3. Fosters inclusivity: Empathy and compassion help us appreciate and celebrate our differences in a diverse world. By recognizing and validating the unique experiences of others, we create an inclusive environment that fosters connection and collaboration.

4. Promotes emotional well-being: Empathetic and compassionate interactions contribute to our emotional well-being and that of others. Feeling understood and supported can boost our mood, reduce stress, and enhance our sense of belonging.

5. Encourages kindness and support: Empathy and compassion can inspire acts of service and support within our circle of friends and family and our broader community. By helping others, we contribute to a more connected and caring society.

While our default capacity for empathy and compassion will vary, they can be developed with practice. As with other foundational skills we have covered in this book, practicing them is beneficial outside of just the scope of this chapter, and you will find many ways to apply these skills in your life.

As always, when practicing a new skill - regardless of what that skill is - find ways to apply it to all areas of your life, especially areas that may at first not seem related. For example, during the lockdown, I entertained myself by learning to play the didgeridoo. It was a fun way to challenge myself with something utterly foreign to my current skill sets, so I chose it. While practicing it, I discovered it would help me better connect with my diaphragm, which had long been a weak area. This would benefit my speaking and singing, which rely on a solid connection to the diaphragm. It also improved my physical exercise routine, helping me better connect to my core and improve in form and performance. Additionally, a year later, when I began trail running to improve my cardio fitness and get outside more, I found that the breathing skills and stronger diaphragm I had been developing in my didgeridoo practice paid off in deeper breathing to support my running. The foundational skills I learned in practicing didgeridoo helped me in ways I had never considered!

The Art of Active Listening

Since practicing active listening has been popping up as a foundational skill in good communication, having personal and professional benefits, we should take this opportunity to delve into this in more detail.

Active listening fully engages in a conversation by listening attentively, understanding, and responding to the speaker, providing verbal and non-verbal feedback to demonstrate genuine interest and empathy.

Here are some ways active listening improves our communication and interpersonal skills and strengthens relationships:

1. Builds trust: When you actively listen to someone, it demonstrates that you genuinely care about their thoughts and feelings. This attention and consideration help to establish trust, which is the foundation of any strong relationship.
2. Enhances understanding: Active listening allows you to understand better the other person's perspective, emotions, and needs. By truly grasping their viewpoint, you can respond more effectively and thoughtfully, strengthening the connection.
3. Encourages open communication: When people feel heard and understood, they are likelier to open up and share their thoughts and feelings. Active listening creates a safe space for open communication, fostering more profound connections.

4. Reduces misunderstandings: By focusing on the speaker and clarifying any confusion, active listening helps prevent misunderstandings, which can otherwise strain relationships.

5. Demonstrates empathy: Active listening involves hearing the words spoken and sensing the emotions behind them. This empathetic understanding can make the other person feel valued and supported, thus strengthening the connection.

6. Makes you likable: When you are genuinely listening and actively engaged with someone, they will usually develop a high regard for you. They may not realize why this is the case since it is often an unconscious observation, but the result is that you are a more likable person.

To practice active listening, consider the following tips:

1. Please give your full attention: When someone is speaking, focus solely on them. Avoid distractions like your phone, and maintain eye contact to show engagement.

2. Show that you're listening: Use verbal and non-verbal cues, such as nodding or saying "I see" or "I understand," to show that you are engaged and attentive. If they are enthusiastic about what they are speaking about, reflect that in your expressions and tone.

3. Reflect and paraphrase: Summarize the speaker's main points in your own words to ensure that you have accurately understood their message. This also gives the speaker a chance to clarify any misconceptions.

4. Ask open-ended questions: Encourage the speaker to elaborate on their thoughts by asking open-ended questions that require more than a simple "yes" or "no" response that can dead-end a conversation. (This can be harder than you may expect! Questions that start with "do," "are," or "can" are best to be rephrased with one of the 5 W's - who, what, where, where, why since that will encourage further elaboration.)

5. Be patient and avoid interrupting: Allow the speaker to finish their thoughts without interjecting, as interruptions can hinder the flow of conversation and make it difficult to establish a deep connection. Are you listening or planning your response?

6. Respond thoughtfully: Once the speaker has finished, take a moment to process their words before responding. Offer

thoughtful feedback, ask follow-up questions, or share your perspective while remaining respectful of their viewpoint.

7. Show empathy and understanding: Acknowledge the speaker's feelings and emotions, even if you do not necessarily agree with their viewpoint. Validate their experiences and demonstrate empathy by saying things like, "I can see why you feel that way" or "That must have been difficult for you."

By practicing active listening, you can create an environment of trust, understanding, and empathy, which is essential in building and maintaining personal and professional relationships, contributing to a more empathetic and compassionate world.

CHAPTER TWELVE

Reconnecting and Building Relationships

The COVID-19 pandemic has highlighted the human connection's crucial role in our well-being. As countries worldwide imposed lockdowns, implemented social distancing measures, and transitioned to remote work or learning, people have faced unprecedented difficulties maintaining social ties. This new reality has sparked an essential discussion on human connection and its mental and emotional health effects.

Pandemic-induced isolation has highlighted our inherent need for social connection and support. With limited access to family, friends, and colleagues, feelings of loneliness, anxiety, and depression have become more frequent. The importance of human connection in maintaining mental health has never been more evident, as many individuals struggle with managing these emotions without their usual social networks. As a result, individuals and communities have had to find creative ways of staying connected - from virtual gatherings to outdoor activities.

Furthermore, the pandemic has highlighted the importance of emotional support and empathy during trying times. Facing a shared threat has fostered an atmosphere of solidarity and compassion among people from different backgrounds. Small acts of kindness like helping neighbors with groceries or volunteering for vulnerable populations have demonstrated how human connection can alleviate hardship and build a more resilient society.

As we navigate the post-pandemic world, reflecting on the lessons learned about the human connection is essential. By cultivating deeper relationships and prioritizing mental health and empathy, we can continue building more robust and supportive communities better equipped to tackle future difficulties.

In this chapter, we'll address the importance of cultivating healthy connections and how we can strengthen existing relationships and forge new ones.

The Importance of Maintaining Connection

Long before the pandemic, there have been plenty of studies demonstrating the power of strong social connections to reduce the risk of depression, and anxiety, among other mental health issues. During the lockdowns of the COVID-19 pandemic, when we suddenly didn't have access to our usual level of human contact, it became all the more apparent how important it is to maintain and nurture those relationships which bring meaning and fulfillment into our lives.

In today's increasingly physical distancing and remote work culture, nurturing our connections to loved ones becomes even more essential for mental well-being and more complex to navigate. Make an effort to reconnect with friends and family members you may have lost touch with during the pandemic; set regular catch-ups, whether in person or virtually; prioritize quality time together; share experiences openly and be an active listener.

Some of the advantages of maintaining healthy relationships include the following:

1. Emotional Well-Being: Healthy relationships offer emotional support, motivation, and a sense of belonging. They assist us through life's ups and downs, contributing to our overall emotional wellness.

2. Counteracting Isolation: With the initial lockdowns of the pandemic and an increase in remote work options, social isolation and loneliness have sharply risen. Through strengthening existing relationships and building new ones, we can help combat these feelings of isolation and create a support network that fosters a sense of community and togetherness.

3. Maintaining Work-Life Balance: With technology increasingly blurring the line between personal and professional lives, it is increasingly important to invest in our relationships to help keep that balance. Spending quality time with family and friends can help reduce stress levels and prevent burnout.

4. Adapting to Change: We face unprecedented rapid changes and uncertainty in the post-pandemic and AI world. But strong relationships provide a secure foundation that allows us to adjust more efficiently and with greater resilience.

5. Collaboration and Innovation: Strong relationships are essential for the successful cooperation in the workplace. In today's increasingly interconnected world, nurturing healthy connections with colleagues is critical for innovation, creativity, and problem-solving.

6. Improving Social Skills: As our communication methods become increasingly digital, finding ways to maintain and develop our social abilities to communicate effectively online and offline becomes even more essential.

7. Enhancing Empathy and Compassion Through Interpersonal Relationships: By cultivating our interpersonal connections, we can foster empathy and compassion within ourselves.

Nurturing and Maintaining Relationships

It is easy to lose sight of the importance of nurturing and maintaining our relationships in today's fast-paced world filled with many distractions and endless responsibilities. We have already discussed how our overall well-being and happiness depend heavily on our relationships with family, friends, and significant others. These relationships offer emotional support, foster personal growth, and contribute to a sense of belonging.

Meaningful relationships are the foundation of a strong sense of community and belonging. To nurture these connections, invest time and energy in your relationships, communicate openly and honestly, and offer support and encouragement to those around you. Be present and engaged during online and in-person interactions, and prioritize quality over quantity when it comes to your social connections.

Nurturing meaningful relationships is vital to fostering community and belonging in a post-pandemic world. As we move forward from the pandemic, it's essential to prioritize and strengthen our connections with others, as these relationships play a crucial role in our overall well-being, happiness, and resilience.

The rest of this chapter is dedicated to exploring some strategies and tips to support you in establishing meaningful, thriving connections.

The Power of Gratitude

In Part 2, we examined how gratitude fosters a positive mindset and helps deepen relationships by creating an atmosphere of love, support, and appreciation. In this section, we'll expand upon that insight by considering the importance of gratitude in building healthy interpersonal connections.

Gratitude can build and foster relationships in several ways:

1. Positive Emotions: Expressing gratitude can produce positive emotions such as happiness, joy, and contentment toward someone. Probably not a shocker here: When we feel positive feelings towards someone, it increases the likelihood that we will have positive interactions and maintain a strong connection.

2. Increased Intimacy: Expressing gratitude towards someone can deepen our feelings of closeness and connection. Expressing our appreciation acknowledges their positive influence in our lives and fosters an atmosphere of appreciation between us.

3. Enhancing communication: Expressing gratitude towards someone can improve communication in relationships. Our expression of thanks serves to express our appreciation for them and their actions, encouraging more positive behavior and improving the interaction between people.

4. Strengthened Commitment: Expressing gratitude towards someone can reinforce our commitments in relationships. Expressing our appreciation for someone's positive influence on us reminds us of their importance in our lives and

strengthens our devotion to the relationship.

5. Greater Resilience: Expressing gratitude towards someone can build more profound and more robust connections by focusing on the positive aspects of a relationship rather than its flaws. This encourages us to adopt a more upbeat outlook and boost our resilience when faced with challenges within that relationship.

To maximize the impact of gratitude in your relationships, try including these practices:

- Reflect on the positive aspects of your connections and experiences with loved ones in a journal - either one dedicated explicitly to gratitude or one that serves other purposes.

- Express gratitude to those in your life through words or thoughtful gestures, either verbally or through meaningful acts. A simple message, phone call, or handwritten note can go a long way toward making someone feel valued and cherished.

- Show your gratitude for others in public settings, such as social media or group gatherings, to demonstrate your admiration and promote positivity.

Prioritizing Quality Over Quantity

When Facebook first gained popularity, some of my friends and associates would boast about how many "friends" they had on the platform. When I finally joined to see what all the fuss was about, I was a bit confused by this concept of "friends" since I kept getting friend requests from strangers who made no effort actually to communicate with me and seemed to be collecting friends purely for the status of a higher count. I would jokingly ask, how many of these "friends" would loan you lunch money if you forgot your wallet?

Similarly, in my younger days, when I would socialize at night clubs, I came to understand the term "club friends." Such friendships typically remain casual or limited to the context of the club or group activities. The challenge is that while these relationships tend to be superficial, we can often mistake that friendly familiarity for a close friendship, only to be disappointed when they are not there to support us in times of need. Of the many club friends I enjoyed spending time with and with whom I have had many an adventure, only a few ended up standing the test of time as actual friends. This is not necessarily bad as long as we recognize their place in our lives. You will see the same phenomenon in organizations and other social groups that bring people together under a common interest, such as sports, hobbies, or professional affiliations, including at the office.

The point of these stories is that quality is more important than quantity regarding human connections. Focus on nurturing a few deep, meaningful relationships rather than fixating on trying to maintain a large number of superficial contacts. Investing time and energy into these relationships will yield greater rewards in terms of emotional support, personal growth, and overall happiness.

When we've experienced social isolation and become increasingly reliant on technology, we must build genuine, meaningful relationships rather than simply expanding our social circles. Investing time and energy in nurturing deeper relationships can create a support network fostering trust, understanding, and resilience. These strong bonds can help you navigate life's challenges, celebrate achievements, and promote a sense of belonging and unity.

Investing in personal growth

Author and motivational speaker Jim Rohn once said, "You are the average of the five people closest to you," a concept that has made its way into many books on personal development and productivity. The premise behind this concept is that the people you spend the most time with significantly influence your thoughts, beliefs, behaviors, and attitudes, thus impacting your overall personal development and productivity.

Seeking out relationships that challenge and inspire one to become the best version of oneself while holding one accountable for one's actions and decisions is essential. These relationships not only contribute to one's personal growth but also provide emotional support, encouragement, and a sense of belonging. You create an environment that encourages growth, learning, and mutual support by surrounding yourself with individuals who share your values and goals.

Encouraging Diversity

Engaging with people from various backgrounds, cultures, and belief systems helps you better understand the world and different viewpoints, increasing cultural awareness and appreciation. This can foster a greater understanding of cultural norms, values, and traditions, helping you become more culturally competent tolerant, and sensitive in your interactions.

Setting and Respecting Boundaries

Boundaries provide guidelines to help one navigate interpersonal relationships, providing a sense of security, autonomy, and mutual understanding. By setting and adhering to boundaries, we create an atmosphere in which both parties feel respected, valued, and supported - ultimately leading to the growth and development of the relationship.

Setting boundaries has many benefits, one of which is the establishment of trust and emotional safety. When people express their needs, preferences, and limits openly, they create a transparent atmosphere where trust can grow. By understanding each other's boundaries and working together to respect them, partners can avoid overstepping or inadvertently causing emotional harm. Furthermore, respecting these boundaries shows both parties are dedicated to the well-being of their relationship while prioritizing each other's emotional needs, further reinforcing trust and increasing emotional intimacy.

Moreover, it helps maintain each individual's sense of autonomy and personal identity within a relationship. Everyone has the right to their thoughts, feelings, and experiences, even in close relationships. Respecting and upholding boundaries allows individuals to retain their sense of self while remaining part of a healthy, fulfilling partnership. This balance of autonomy and connection encourages personal growth and development, ensuring that both parties can continue to contribute positively to the relationship in the long run. Ultimately, setting and respecting boundaries is essential in nurturing healthy relationships and cultivating emotional well-being for all individuals involved.

Due to the increasingly blurry boundaries between work and personal life with the popularization of remote work and education, many people have been spending an unprecedented amount of time with family members or partners, leading to potential boundary issues and conflicts. As we all seek to find our sense of equilibrium in this "new normal," we must remember that these struggles are real.

Here are some tips to support setting, communicating, and respecting healthy boundaries:

1. Communicate Your Needs Openly and Honestly: Communicate your feelings, needs, and expectations with those closest to you. This facilitates mutual respect's boundaries and leads to more harmonious interactions.

2. Be assertive yet respectful: Be confident to stand up for yourself and respectfully express your boundaries. Remember that it's okay to say no or decline invitations that don't align with your priorities or values.

3. Organize Your Schedule Mindfully: Establish specific times for work, personal relationships, and self-care. Doing this helps you maintain a healthy work-life balance and ensure you have dedicated time for nurturing relationships without feeling overwhelmed.

4. Create technology boundaries with kindness: Set limits on using devices and social media during personal or family time to prioritize face-to-face interactions. Establish tech-free zones or times, and encourage others to do the same for a deeper connection with loved ones and at work. A practice one of my close friends keeps when dining out is to have everyone place their phones in the center of the table so that everyone is more present during the meal.

5. Prioritize self-care: Set aside time for activities that nourish your mind, body, and soul. By prioritizing yourself, you can bring the best version of yourself to your relationships - radiating positivity and warmth from within.

6. Maintain emotional boundaries with compassion: Show support to others without taking on their problems or emotions as your own. Doing this allows you to safeguard your emotional well-being while being there for those you care about.

7. Respect Others' Boundaries with Understanding: Acknowledge and respect the boundaries set by others while

encouraging an open dialogue about each other's needs and expectations. Mutual respect is the cornerstone of a healthy, vibrant relationship. When unsure about a boundary, ask.

8. Reevaluate Boundaries Periodically with Flexibility: Evaluating and adjusting your boundaries is essential as life circumstances evolve. Keep the lines of communication open and remain adaptable for your relationships to thrive.

9. Lead by example: Model healthy boundary setting and encourage others to do the same. Your actions can serve as a positive example for those around you.

Implementing these strategies will enable you to create boundaries that nurture and protect existing relationships, foster mutual respect, facilitate open communication, and promote emotional and mental health - leading to more satisfying, authentic connections.

Prioritizing Communication

Even before the pandemic, social media had complicated communication in our modern lives. One can build a solid foundation for mutual understanding, support, and growth by prioritizing communication in one's relationships. These efforts lead to more robust and rewarding connections with those necessary in one's life that last long-term.

Here are some ways communication can be prioritized to build and strengthen relationships:

1. Encourage open and honest dialogue: Foster trust by candidly conversing with friends, family members, or colleagues. Transparency about one's thoughts and feelings helps build connections and fosters a climate where everyone feels heard and understood.

2. Active Listening: Demonstrate active listening by giving the other your full attention, asking questions, and reflecting on what they have said. Doing this demonstrates your genuine interest in their opinions and views, creating stronger bonds.

3. Empathy and Understanding: When communicating with others, try to put yourself in their shoes and understand their emotions and perspectives. This approach helps create a supportive and caring atmosphere in your relationships.

4. Regular Check-Ins: Make an effort to check in with those in your life regularly, even just a quick text or phone call. Show that you genuinely care about their well-being and want to maintain an authentic connection.

5. Conflict Resolution: Conflicts and misunderstandings are inevitable in any relationship. Prioritizing communication allows one to address issues head-on, find solutions, and strengthen their bonds by working through problems together.

6. Express Gratitude and Appreciation: Make it a habit of expressing gratitude and admiration for those in your life, whether through verbal affirmations or small gestures like sending a thank-you note. Demonstrating appreciation breeds positive feelings and helps to reinforce the value of your relationships.

7. Adjust Your Communication Style: Every person has a preferred communication style. By adapting yours to meet the needs of others, you show respect and consideration for their preferences, ultimately leading to stronger connections.

8. Non-verbal Communication: Remember that communication is not only words but also non-verbal cues like body language, tone of voice, and facial expressions. Be aware of these signals, as they can shape how your message is received and understood.

9. Quality Time: Make time for meaningful interactions with those closest to you. Spending quality time together helps strengthen your bond and provides chances for meaningful conversations.

10. Emotional Support: Offer your loved ones a listening ear and emotional support during difficult times. Being present for them during these trying times strengthens your bond and trust.

Being Authentic

Staying true to one's core values, beliefs, and emotions plays a crucial role in cultivating deeper connections, personal growth, and emotional well-being. By being true to ourselves, we create an environment where relationships can thrive and find greater fulfillment in our lives.

Being authentic cultivates genuine connections with others. By being true to ourselves, we attract those who share our values and perspectives; this builds trust and intimacy that allows for open communication and emotional intimacy. Genuine connection is essential for maintaining long-lasting and fulfilling relationships as it fosters mutual understanding, respect, and support. Ultimately people will sense, consciously or not, when you are not projecting authenticity and will generally distrust those who seem lacking.

By accepting our true selves, we become more self-aware and sensitive to our feelings, desires, and needs. This increased self-awareness enables us to make wiser decisions, set appropriate boundaries, and develop a strong sense of identity. Moreover, by acknowledging both strengths and weaknesses, we can work towards improving ourselves and becoming the best version of ourselves possible. Embracing authenticity thus fosters self-worth and confidence by enabling us to pursue passions without external pressures or expectations from society or external pressures.

Finally, being authentic contributes to our overall emotional well-being. When we suppress or hide our true emotions in order to fit social norms, it can often lead to feelings of isolation, inadequacy, and discontentment. However, by being true to ourselves, we grant ourselves permission to feel all positive and negative emotions without judgment or self-censorship. This emotional honesty promotes self-compassion, resilience, and inner peace, leading to a more rewarding and balanced life overall.

Fostering a Sense of Community and Belonging

It's easy to blame the pandemic for causing the widespread loneliness, disconnection, and uncertainty many of us face today. While it certainly added to the situation, this growing trend of disconnection, ironically in an age where we are so connected via our technology, has been an increasing concern, even before the crisis of the pandemic hit.

For example, before the pandemic, recent studies showed a decline in friendships in modern society and increasing feelings of loneliness and isolation, which have been taking their toll on well-being, increasing the risk for mental health problems. Unfortunately, the pandemic only compounded this trend. On the positive side, we are finally discussing this concern.

It has been suggested that the causes of this general decline in friendship could be attributed to several factors:

1. Technology: The growth of technology has made it easier to connect with others online, yet this also leads to a decline in face-to-face interactions. People may spend more time on social media or messaging apps, yet these virtual connections offer a different intimacy level than face-to-face encounters.

2. Busy Lifestyles: Many people today lead hectic lives, with work and family commitments taking up much of their time. This makes it challenging to find the energy to invest in friendships or form new connections.

3. Mobility: People today are more mobile than ever, often moving for work or personal reasons. This makes it difficult to maintain existing friendships or forge new ones. This was further exasperated during the pandemic when many moved out of cities.

4. Individualism: There has been a cultural shift towards individualism in recent years, with people focusing more on their goals and desires than social connections. This makes it challenging to prioritize friendships and maintain healthy relationships.

5. Changes in Society: Recent societal changes, such as the decline of community organizations and the rise of online shopping and entertainment, have resulted in decreased social connections and a sense of belonging.

6. Growing Polarization in Politics and Other Beliefs: The news bubbles created by social media algorithms to keep viewers engaged have led to more significant division among "sides," widening the gap between those with differing viewpoints and fostering an "us vs. them" mentality.

Community and belonging are essential for our well-being and personal growth. Connecting with others can build strong social networks, foster our sense of purpose, and create a supportive environment to thrive. As we close out this chapter, we will examine the significance of belonging and how we can foster a sense of community and belonging to support our collective well-being.

Connecting with Like-Minded Individuals

Before the pandemic, I conversed with my coaching colleague about the difficulties of making friends after college. Back then, peers with similar interests and activities at school constantly surrounded us. There were numerous ways to connect and be introduced to others, from clubs and parties to simply hanging out in common areas. As soon as we graduated and stepped into the workplace, everything changed. Our focus shifted to building a career, and while some of us may have had friendly conversations with colleagues at work, those connections rarely extend outside of the office.

Our old circle of friends slowly faded as life took them in different directions. People moved, married, or found new priorities. Finding new connections became a task, and unfortunately, I often don't feel motivated to put forth that effort anymore to make new friends, and I know I am not alone in that sentiment. I sometimes wonder whether this disinterest is a byproduct of my isolation or whether I genuinely enjoy my time at home. If I am honest with myself, it is probably a bit of both. Unfortunately, that leaves me with a shrinking pool of people to call on when seeking companionship or support.

Finding like-minded individuals with shared interests, values, or goals can foster a strong sense of community and belonging. Surrounding ourselves with people who share our interests, values, and passions will enrich our lives and create a more resilient and supportive society.

Here are some helpful strategies to assist you in discovering and connecting with like-minded individuals:

1. Explore Your Interests and Passions: Take time to pause and reflect on the hobbies, values, and goals that drive you. By identifying activities or causes that excite you, connecting with like-minded individuals with whom you can form meaningful connections will become easier.

2. Join clubs or organizations: Get involved in local clubs, community organizations, or social groups that align with

your interests or values. These gatherings allow you to connect with new people, learn from others, and contribute toward shared objectives.

3. Attend Events and Workshops: Keep an eye out for events, workshops, or conferences related to your interests - both online and off. These gatherings offer a great chance to network with like-minded individuals, expand your knowledge base, and develop new skills.

4. Utilize Social Media and Online Platforms: Utilize social media, online forums, and platforms like Meetup to discover and connect with people who share your interests. Participate in relevant online communities, join discussions, and engage in conversations to foster connections.

5. Volunteer for a Cause: Donate your time and energy to causes that matter by volunteering for nonprofit organizations, community projects, or local events. Not only does volunteering make an impact, but it also brings together like-minded people who share your enthusiasm for making things better.

6. Create Your Own Group or Initiative: If you can't find a group or organization that meets your interests, why not start one yourself? This way, you control the group's direction and provide an outlet for those with similar passions to come together.

7. Be approachable and open: When engaging with others, strive to be positive, approachable, and willing to listen. Doing this will inspire others to connect with you and make it simpler for like-minded people to form connections.

8. Prioritize maintaining connections: friendships and community relationships require time and attention, or they will eventually fade away. Set aside time each day to nurture these essential connections.

The Hard Truth

While sharing ideas on how to find and connect with others is beneficial, remember that friendships don't just happen. They require effort, time, energy, and a commitment to maintaining them - something our busy lives often don't allow for. Nowadays, getting distracted from our connections is far too easy, which has had unfortunate repercussions. Prioritizing and maintaining our relationships will go a long way toward providing us with a reliable support system when needed most.

An analogy could be to consider houseplant care. Plants require regular care - watering, pruning, and moving to larger pots for growth as needed. While it doesn't take a lot of effort, one must commit enough time each week to provide enough care for the plant to flourish.

CHAPTER THIRTEEN

Happiness

Early in my career as an IT professional, I was responsible for supporting the VIPs of my employer at the time. These were very wealthy people... *very* rich. I won't name names, but one lived in a massive apartment in the Waldorf Astoria (a luxurious hotel in New York City) with marble and hardwood floors and a gigantic farm estate in upstate NY. Another lived on Park Avenue in Manhattan, his apartment extending two floors, and yet another lived outside the city in a beautiful home in a very exclusive area. As a young striving professional dealing with debt and having his share of difficult times growing up, these people seemed to have it all, living "the good life." They were driven to work, went to exotic places for vacation, mingled with the rich and famous, and some even had helicopters and yachts.

Since I was often working on their computers and other technology both at home and in the office while they were absorbed in their work and also assisted their family, friends, and sometimes lovers, I had the opportunity to experience glimpses of their daily lives, usually unnoticed or ignored as I fumbled with wires behind a desk or an open PC in the corner. What I discovered was... confusing.

These wealthy people were often very unhappy, dealing with the same drama as the "regular schmoe." There were messy divorces, crazy or manipulative lovers, petty grievances, family complications, health issues... the list went on. The people living what I thought was the perfect life were like the rest of us. This same message came to me repeatedly as I saw headlines of the famous and their woes in the news.

Fame, money, and material objects were not enough for happiness. Money could help remove some of my current obstacles and sources of stress, but there would always be others to take their place. I wish I had taken this valuable discovery to heart then, but I did not.

Later in life, when I was more professionally successful, financially better off, and even a little well-known in certain circles, I slipped into depression. Here I was at the pinnacle of my success and was unhappy. I wanted to be happy, but it became clear to me I did not know what happiness was. I had been clinging to a flawed notion of happiness, and this was not leading me any closer to it. It was making me more unhappy. It was then that I decided it was time to understand better what happiness was.

The Happiness Fallacies

Before we can understand the true nature of happiness, we need to recognize and let go of the fallacies that are getting in the way. One would think happiness would not be such a complex subject, but as I discovered when I decided a few years ago to find ways of bringing more joy to my own life, our inaccurate assumptions about happiness can lead us in the opposite direction! These are the stealthy robbers and saboteurs of happiness lurking in our beliefs and expectations.

Below are examples of what happiness is NOT...

Happiness is Not Feeling Good All the Time

As humans, we are not in a static state. We constantly respond physically, mentally, and emotionally to external and internal experiences, thoughts, and perceptions (consciously or not). Our body chemistry, which can influence mood, will vary with diet, environment, and one's present emotional state. We are always in flux but cling to the illusion of a static sense of self.

Thus our capacity and receptiveness to happiness can vary throughout our lives and even the day. Furthermore, when you ask people what makes their lives worth living, they rarely say anything about their mood. They are more likely to cite things that they find meaningful, such as their work, relationships, assets, or experiences.

Research suggests that if you focus too much on *trying* to feel good all the time, you'll undermine your ability to feel good. Essentially, if you expect to feel good all the time, no amount will satisfy you since we cannot realistically sustain such a constant state in our current condition as humans. Likewise, if you focus on the peaks, you will dread the inevitable decline, or for that matter, the needed effort to get to that peak, to begin with. This can lead to escapism through drugs or other mind-altering or distracting habits, which further rob us of opportunities for happiness.

Happiness is Not Just in Your Head

The idea that our thinking influences our emotions is nothing new. You will find plenty of books and systems on happiness and personal success that focus on or are inspired by the principle that happiness is purely a matter of changing our thoughts. As we will explore in this section, it is true that our thought patterns play a significant role in our sense of well-being and capacity for resilience (or lack thereof). However, it paints an incomplete picture, and we must acknowledge another key player: meeting our emotional and physical needs and honoring our values. We have an instinctual desire to fill these needs, and when they are not met, we will feel anxiety. Life can feel meaningless when we do not act in ways that honor our values. So identifying and meeting these needs and values will contribute to our overall happiness and allow us to focus on how our thoughts also play a role here.

I am reminded of Maslow's Hierarchy of Needs. The general gist of this theory is that our various needs fall into a hierarchy of priorities most often displayed as a pyramid where the needs at the base are essentially one's basic physical requirements (food, water, sleep, warmth, etc.). Only once these lower-level needs have been met can we move on to the next level of needs, which in this model would cover safety and security. Needs that involve personal growth are much further up in this pyramid. So to have the luxury of exploring how to shift one's mode of thinking to be more supportive of happiness, we would probably first need to take care of the more pressing basic needs. If you are worried about your next meal or how to pay off crushing debt, you have no motivation to explore your thought patterns and their impact on your well-being.

This is extremely important to recognize since it contributes to the dark side of personal growth and happiness, where it is often packaged as a luxury item. The materials (books, articles, courses, etc.) typically assume one has their basic needs met, so they can be marketed and presented in ways that take them out of reach of the less fortunate. A low-income parent trying to juggle education and work and wanting to better themselves can feel overlooked and stuck in a situation where their basic needs are not being met enough to allow them to focus on more. Worse, focusing only on the thinking aspects of happiness can make those struggling with their basic needs feel like something is wrong with them since they cannot escape the anxiety of not meeting their basic needs. *Anxiety, stress, and depression cannot be thought away any more than thirst can be thought away for someone needing hydration.* These feelings are instinctual responses to the current lack of basic needs.

So happiness also depends upon our environment and experiences and how we make sense of them. It is not purely in one's mind.

Happiness is Not About Being Rich

At the beginning of this section, I already spoke at length about this discovery, so I will only add a few points here to consider.

Studies have shown that while living below the poverty line certainly makes it hard to be happy, beyond that, money does not appear to increase happiness. The excitement from things like getting a big raise, buying a new house, car, gadget, or all of the other material goods people spend so much time pining over is short-term. It is a matter of time before your expectations change to fit your new budget or environment. Before you know it, you're just as happy (or unhappy) as you were before!

There is, however, an exception to this rule. You might become happier when you spend your time or money on *experiences*, especially with other people. However, even here, it is not about the amount of money spent but rather about the enjoyable experiences themselves.

Happiness is Not A Final Destination

I used to think I would be happy if I could pay off my debt. And when I finally did, I was… for a little while. That success did not keep me happy forever; it simply removed one of the sources that made me unhappy. There will always be new challenges to face. Holding happiness out like a carrot to lead us to it will never bring us to an end. We will never "get there" since it was never a final destination, to begin with.

Contrary to popular belief, it takes regular effort to maintain happiness unless you are one of the few who won the genetic lottery and are naturally happy. Most established techniques for becoming happier (which we will explore soon!) are habits, not one-shot events. Most life events that make us happy in the short term, like getting married or being promoted, fade over time as we adapt to them.

Happiness Does Not Have To Be Huge

If I were to describe my most content and happy moment in the past year, you may not be impressed. I was sitting on the couch at home working on some random task on my laptop with two of my adopted cats on either side of me, purring contently. As I looked down at them with a smile, one looked back, reached out to gently touch me with its paw as it stretched, and then nuzzled closer to drift off to slumber, lightly purring with a long, contented sigh. It was the perfect moment, and as I think back to it now, I cannot help but smile and feel a bit of that happiness return as a lingering warm glow - such a simple yet potent event in my life and one I experience regularly. Since I adopted my cats, they have made me smile every day without fail for years. I smile when I think of them, and I smile when I come home from work. I am smiling as I write this.

I can think back to when my career started to take off, and I was promoted to my first management position, which almost doubled my salary. It immediately resolved my money issues at the time, and I was 100% debt free within a year. I was proud and excited, but it did not take long to adjust to my new salary, move to a better apartment, and eventually buy a house. The happiness of that event was a peak moment that faded quickly. If I look back, I recall it being a pivotal moment in my career, but I have new issues and demands which need attending. That peak no longer has relevance to me. It no longer brings me joy.

While these peaks are not without value, it is often the seemingly "little things" which can stay with us. Do not underestimate their contribution to your long-term happiness.

Happiness is Not "Out There"

As cliché as it sounds, happiness comes from within. The more we objectify happiness as something external to be obtained, the more we will lose sight of it. The more we relegate happiness to "if only…" the more we distance ourselves from it.

We are ultimately the source of our happiness or lack thereof. Every time we project the cause onto others, we disempower ourselves in the process. For example, I can't control when someone is rude on the subway, but I can choose how to perceive and respond. I can't always maintain my environment, but when my basic needs are not being met, I can either choose to wallow in that condition or take on the struggle to meet those needs.

Additionally, if I create external dependencies for my happiness (getting recognition or validation, having things, etc.), I limit my opportunities and create disappointment.

If we wish to be happy, we need to take responsibility for our happiness and lack thereof. Only then can we begin to take steps to increase our joy.

So, Then, What IS Happiness?

Happiness combines how satisfied one is with one's life (for example, finding meaning in one's work and relationships) and how good one feels daily. When we are resilient, both are relatively stable in that, while our life circumstances change and our mood fluctuates, we inevitably return to a general baseline of happiness.

We each have our base level and capacity for happiness hardwired at birth. However, do not fret if you feel your base level could be better. The good news is, with consistent effort, this can be offset. Consider your health when it comes to diet and exercise. If we did not put much effort into this, some of us might get fat, others may remain lanky, and others seem to be in great shape even without the effort (those bastards!!!). Each of us would have different considerations for diet and exercise to look and feel healthier. The more consistent the effort put in, the better the results. If I eat poorly all week and only diet well on weekends, my progress will be much slower. And if we stop our effort altogether, we will eventually return to a similar state from which we started. If you lost weight, you would gain it back. If you had built muscle, you would lose it.

It is the same when it comes to happiness. We may have a default baseline, but we can control how we choose to respond to setbacks, and with consistent practice, we can form lifelong habits for a more satisfying and fulfilling life. You can take control of your happiness to a great extent by taking conscious ownership of one's thoughts, behaviors, and actions.

We cannot change the genes we were born with or undo past trauma, but we can change ourselves through our choices and habits and choose how to move forward.

How Do We Increase Our Happiness?

What one repeatedly spends time thinking about and doing each day ultimately forms the person one is, the things one believes, and the personality that one portrays. So in seeking to find happiness, we must take an honest (and forgiving) look inward. As the saying goes, happiness comes from within.

Start with the Basics

As I mentioned above in the section on the facilities of happiness, it is difficult for one to be happy if we are not meeting our basic needs and living a life that honors our values. Take advantage of the material in part one of this book to better understand one's core needs, values, and passions. In part four, we will be adding to that list our strengths. All of this information plays directly into our happiness and well-being.

Reflect on these questions:
- Are you meeting your needs?
- Do your work and lifestyle honor the values you find most important?
- Are you aligning your life and work with your passions?
- Are you leveraging your strengths?

If you are not answering these with a confident "yes!" then this would be the first place to begin to review to see what changes can be made to improve your situation.

The Little Things Matter

Consider a rope. A rope is a collection of smaller strands twisted together. Each strand cannot hold much weight, but they manifest the rope's strength together. To bring more happiness into one's life, find ways of incorporating various "little things" as habits that each bring more and more joy and cultivate resilience to unexpected challenges.

Some of these seemingly "little things" may surprise you in their effectiveness. Take a break from social media feeds for a week, for example. It probably won't be easy, but you may be surprised at the peace of mind it can bring once you get past the withdrawal symptoms of that addiction.

The more we develop habits conducive to happiness and discover and deal with habits that sabotage our happiness and success, the more satisfied we will become.

Hone Skills That Will Further Your Efforts

This book explores many general skills that are both valuable and can serve as helpful tools in any area of your life you choose to work on. Determining what is important to us by reflecting on our needs and values, and learning to become more mindful, resilient, and compassionate, for example, would greatly help one's efforts to increase happiness.

Maintaining a journal can offer excellent insight into the patterns one's habits and lifestyle create and how they impact one's mood.

As you explore various tips on bringing more happiness into your life, consider what underlying skills such tips rely on. The more you can find practical ways to apply the ideas presented in the book, the more accessible those skills will be in future endeavors.

The Dark Side of Happiness

Beyond the often-repeated caution that the more one strives for happiness, the further away you'll end up, I believe several trappings are essential to recognize.

First and foremost, happiness is subjective. What brings me joy may be stressful or uninteresting to someone else. A group of friends once joined me for a night of camping in the woods after seeing my eyes light up when talking about sitting by the fire sipping tea or watching the moon's slow journey across the sky from my hammock. It sounded so magical to them. The reality was a bit different, and they ended up spending a sleepless night inside their tent, frightened by all of nature's sounds in the dark and experiencing nothing but regret! City folk, what can I say?

Follow your interests and passions. Draw inspiration from others, but remember: what works for someone else may not necessarily work for you or even be conducive to your well-being.

Happiness doesn't always look perfect or worthy of Instagram. Maybe you are not in a position to witness a sunset in Antarctica, but you can certainly find a local scenic spot and enjoy it from there. The most amazing sunset I have ever witnessed - one that left me speechless and pondering the wonders of life - was in the back of a warehouse on the edge of an industrial park. At that moment, the dumpsters and drab architecture around me faded amidst my wonder of the profound.   When we wait for perfection, we miss all the opportunities for joy and wonder right before us.

Finally, a word of caution regarding toxic positivity. This mindset refers to the excessive or forced promotion of a positive outlook, often at the expense of acknowledging genuine emotions - especially negative ones. It implies that one should maintain a positive outlook regardless of circumstances and that negative emotions are undesirable or harmful. Phrases like "just think positive," "everything happens for a reason," or "look on the bright side" can diminish or trivialize someone's struggles, pain, or negative emotions.

By insisting on positivity at all times, toxic positivity encourages the suppression of negative emotions, leading to increased stress, anxiety, and a decline in mental health. Happiness and positivity don't have to mean being always happy; there will be times when we need to grieve, worry, or be angry, for example. Our resilience developed from cultivating positivity and self-care should enable us to acknowledge these genuine experiences without becoming consumed with negative self-talk. Neglecting genuine feelings or experiences can leave people feeling invalidated, unsupported, and isolated, negatively impacting overall happiness and well-being.

Genuine happiness requires accepting and understanding the full range of human emotions while understanding that negative ones have their place and can serve as catalysts for growth and self-awareness. By encouraging emotional honesty and validating others' experiences, we can promote an authentic approach to happiness that doesn't rely on superficial positivity alone.

Part 4

Career and Professional Life

CHAPTER FOURTEEN

Professional Assessment and Image

Embarking on the journey to develop a professional image supporting your career path begins with a deep understanding of oneself. In this chapter, we will explore the process of identifying your strengths and opportunities for growth, laying the groundwork for crafting an authentic and powerful professional image and mission statement. Knowing your capabilities and areas for improvement will enable you to represent your professional self authentically and resonate with your target audience, helping set you apart in a crowded job market.

Through self-assessment and introspection, you'll uncover the distinct attributes that define you and what you bring to the workplace. We will delve into various techniques and tools designed to help you gain clarity on your core strengths and "weaknesses," transforming these insights into a foundation for your professional image. With a clear understanding of your strengths, you'll be well-equipped to develop a professional image that aligns with your goals, values, and passions.

As you progress through this chapter, you'll learn how to embrace your strengths and identify and leverage growth opportunities, using them to shape your professional image and create a compelling narrative that captures the essence of your professional identity. Once you've spent some time in self-discovery and built a solid professional image and mission statement, the next chapter will guide you through reevaluating your career path, ensuring it aligns with your newly refined image to support your long-term aspirations. Together, these chapters will empower you to take control of your professional journey, leveraging your authentic professional image to achieve greater success and satisfaction in your chosen field.

Your work in part one of this book - identifying your needs, values, and passion - will prove an invaluable prerequisite. If you have not worked through that process yet, I encourage you to invest some time into that now before proceeding further. We will soon add to those insights by identifying your strengths and opportunities for growth.

Identifying Strengths and Opportunities

This process is often called Identifying Strengths and Weaknesses, but I dislike using the word "weakness." It focuses too much on what's lacking instead of finding areas for improvement. From a growth mindset perspective, any weakness should be seen as an opportunity to develop new abilities.

As you progress in your career, taking time to assess where you stand and identify your strengths and potential growth areas is essential. Doing this will enable you to recognize areas for improvement and maximize the use of all of your talents and abilities. Jobs that don't leverage your strengths and lack challenge and engagement likely won't provide long-term satisfaction, even if the paycheck is substantial.

Identifying one's strengths is a beneficial exercise to include in one's journal or even keep a separate notebook solely dedicated to documenting and planning one's career development.

Step 1: Conduct a Self-Assessment

The initial step in understanding your strengths and weaknesses is conducting a self-assessment. This entails an honest assessment of skills, experience, and knowledge to pinpoint what you excel at and struggle with most.

Reflect on the following questions:

Strengths:

- What tasks or projects do I enjoy doing most?
- What tasks or projects have I received the most positive feedback on?

- What skills do I possess that set me apart from others or allow me to excel in certain areas more than others at my workplace?
- What tasks or projects am I better at than others in my workplace?
- Which abilities would most benefit my employer if I acquired them?
- What accomplishments or successes am I most proud of, and what do my colleagues or superiors often commend me on?
- Which tasks or responsibilities do I feel most confident handling?

Opportunities:
- What areas of my workplace do I feel less confident or skilled in than other employees?
- What tasks or responsibilities do I struggle with?
- Which projects do I find enjoyable?
- Have I received any feedback in performance evaluations that indicates areas for improvement?
- What training or development opportunities have I avoided because they require more skill?
- Are there any patterns in my work habits or behaviors that might hinder my career growth?
- What knowledge or experience do I lack that could limit my career growth?

By answering these questions honestly and objectively, you'll gain a clearer picture of your strengths and potential avenues for improvement.

Step 2: Seek Feedback from Others

In addition to self-assessment, seeking feedback from others can help you recognize your strengths and identify areas that could use improvement. This could come from peers, mentors, or supervisors who have worked with you and have a better insight into your capabilities and potential. It is essential to leverage this outside perspective since we often miss details due to our unconscious biases.

Reflect on the following questions:

Strengths:
- What do I do exceptionally well?
- What sets me apart in our workplace environment?

- Are there any tasks or projects where you believe I excel over my colleagues?
- What do you consider my most significant contributions to the team or company?
- What strengths could I leverage more?

Opportunities:

- How could I improve my performance in my current role?
- What tasks or responsibilities could benefit from additional training or development?
- Are there any patterns in my work habits or behaviors that might hinder me professionally?
- What feedback have you provided me in the past that you think I could benefit from revisiting?
- Are there any tasks or responsibilities where you believe I need more support or guidance to be successful?
- What opportunities would help me grow professionally?
- Are there areas in which I could benefit from additional training?
- Where am I holding myself back?
- If I could improve one thing, what would it be?

You'll better understand how others view your strengths and where you could improve by seeking feedback. Stay open-minded here and take advantage of their unique perspectives. If someone says something that doesn't agree with you, instead of disputing that point or defending yourself, explore why an outside observer might have formed that perception. For instance, my quietness can be misconstrued as disinterest or even grumpiness by those around me, so I try to be mindful of that and know that when lost in thought, I can appear unapproachable, so I make a point to smile when making eye contact with someone.

Additionally, if you experience a strong emotional response to feedback, reflect on it. An intense emotion often indicates something important being learned here; note how you interpreted that feedback. What was significant about that experience? What needed improving?

Step 3: Evaluate Your Accomplishments

Reflect on positive feedback and examine past projects or tasks you've completed. Note what went well and which skills were essential to success. Remember to celebrate and recognize these accomplishments - they deserve recognition!

Ask yourself the following questions:

- What projects or tasks have I completed that I am most proud of?
- What skills or knowledge did I utilize to ensure success on these initiatives?
- What are some examples of when I went above and beyond my job duties to ensure success on a project?
- Have I received any accolades or recognition for my work on this project? If so, what was the project, and what precisely did I contribute?
- Can I recall a time when I overcame an obstacle or challenge to achieve success on a project or task?
- Which projects/tasks am I particularly proud of and why?
- Have I received positive feedback or praise from colleagues, clients, or superiors regarding any specific initiatives?

By reviewing your accomplishments, you'll be able to recognize your strengths and how they have contributed to your professional success.

Step 4: Review Your Setbacks

While dwelling on one's setbacks, failures, and obstacles is counterproductive, acknowledging them and what role we play is essential if we want to turn these disappointments into opportunities for growth. As previously discussed in the book, success comes from learning and adapting from mistakes; failure is inevitable but doesn't need to be in vain! Be honest with yourself but also forgiving.

Ask yourself these questions:

- Are there any projects or tasks I struggled with or didn't complete to the best of my ability?
- Can I identify any areas where I lacked the knowledge or skills necessary for complete success on a project or task?
- What challenges or obstacles were encountered during this endeavor that proved difficult to overcome?
- Have I experienced negative feedback or criticism from colleagues, clients, or superiors regarding a project?
- Which projects or tasks have I avoided because I feel less

confident or capable in those areas?

Step 5: Craft a Personal Development Plan

Once you've identified your strengths and areas that could improve, creating a personal development plan will support you in taking needed action. This should contain the steps you'll take to build upon these attributes and maximize yourself by acting upon identified opportunities for growth.

Consider taking these steps:

1. Create a plan of action to seize an opportunity for growth or utilize an underutilized strength.
2. Determine which training or development opportunities you should take advantage of.
3. Set goals that are Specific, Measurable, Achievable, Relevant, and Time-bound (SMART).
4. Track progress by setting checkpoints to assess progress toward reaching specific objectives.
5. Maintain your personal development plan regularly to guarantee its relevance and efficacy. As your career progresses, goals and needs may evolve, necessitating changes to the development plan accordingly.

When I was new as a manager, I often struggled to stay organized and on track when I first became responsible for projects and deadlines. Tracking progress and delegating tasks weren't my strong suit. I took an online project management course that year and applied its lessons to my next project, documenting my progress. Utilizing a project management tool helped me keep track of who I had assigned what, and I made a point to delegate any tasks I did not need to do personally. Each new project was an opportunity to practice these newly acquired skills.

Establishing a personal development plan allows you to build upon your strengths and seize growth opportunities proactively.

Leveraging Your Strengths

We often focus on addressing weaknesses during assessments, so be sure also to remember to consider your strengths. Once you've identified your strengths, consider how they can be utilized in your career.

- Are there roles or industries where your strengths are beneficial?
- Can you seek out new opportunities that enable you to utilize them more efficiently?
- Do any of your assets set you apart from the competition?
- What abilities are currently underutilized, and where could they be better utilized?
- How can you further build upon or develop your strengths?

You'll be better prepared to create a rewarding and successful career by building on your strengths and setting objectives that address growth opportunities, including ones that help amplify or better utilize your strengths and talents.

Developing a Personal Mission Statement

A personal mission statement concisely expresses your core values, purpose, and aspirations and develops a clear professional image. It serves as a guiding framework for your personal and professional life, reflecting your vision for the future and the impact you want to make. It can help you make decisions, set goals, and determine your priorities, all while staying true to your beliefs and identity. The personal mission statement gives your professional image context and helps provide focus on one's career path.

Craft a concise message communicating your value, passion, and expertise. To create a cohesive and memorable impression, your professional image should be consistent across all channels, including your resume, social media profiles, and personal website.

The personal mission statement contributes to your career path in the following ways:

- Authenticity: A well-crafted personal mission statement ensures your public image remains authentic to your core values. It helps you maintain consistency in your actions and decisions, reinforcing the integrity of your professional image.
- Direction and focus: Your mission statement provides a clear path and focus for your professional image, helping you concentrate your efforts on the goals and values that matter most to you. This focus enables you to make more effective

decisions, allocate resources efficiently, and pursue opportunities that align with your mission.

- Target audience connection: A personal mission statement can help you resonate with your target audience by revealing your underlying motivations, aspirations, and principles. When your audience understands your "why," they are likelier to trust, connect with, and invest in you.
- Long-term vision: Your mission statement represents your long-term vision and purpose, which can be essential in building a sustainable professional image and career path. You demonstrate dedication, resilience, and commitment to your professional image by continuously working towards your mission.

To create your mission statement, consider the following steps:

1. Reflect on your core values: Identify the principles and beliefs that guide your life and shape your decisions. These values will form the foundation of your mission statement.

2. Define your purpose: Consider the impact you want to make and the legacy you want to leave. Use your skills, passions, and strengths to make a difference in your field, industry, or community.

3. Set long-term goals: Establish the goals you want to achieve personally and professionally. These goals should align with your values and purpose and provide a clear direction for your career path.

4. Craft a concise statement: Combine your core values, purpose, and long-term goals into a clear and concise statement that effectively communicates your mission. Keep your message focused and understandable, ensuring it resonates with your target audience.

Here are some examples of personal mission statements for various professions and goals:

- Graphic Designer: "To use my creative talents and technical skills to produce visually stunning designs that inspire, engage, and leave a lasting impact on clients and their audiences."
- Digital Marketer: "To empower businesses to achieve their full potential by implementing data-driven marketing strategies

that fuel growth, build brand awareness, and foster lasting customer relationships."

- Career Coach: "To guide and support individuals in discovering their true passions, unlocking their potential, and achieving career success through personalized coaching and actionable strategies."
- Web Developer: "To create innovative, user-centric web solutions that elevate the online presence of businesses, enhance user experience, and contribute to the growth and success of the digital world."
- Content Writer: "To craft compelling stories that educate, entertain, and inspire, using the power of the written word to connect with readers and make a positive impact on their lives."

When crafting your mission statement, focus on your core values, purpose, and long-term goals. Ensure that it is concise, easy to understand, and effectively communicates the impact you want to make in your field or industry. A compelling personal mission statement can guide your career path and support your professional image, enabling you to stay true to your values and aspirations while resonating with your target audience.

CHAPTER FIFTEEN

Assessing One's Career Path

Recent years have witnessed a dramatic transformation in our world. The pandemic disrupted lives and careers, while advances in AI and other technologies continue to alter how we work and live, adding much uncertainty with future opportunities. To stay adaptable, resilient, and creative during such uncertainty, it helps to take the time now to assess one's current position and plan for one's career goals.

In this chapter, we'll take you through a step-by-step process designed to help you assess and reorient your career path in this rapidly evolving landscape. By the end, you'll have the tools to craft an individualized career path that aligns with your strengths, interests, and aspirations while creating a roadmap that provides direction and focus as you proceed. Your work in the previous chapter to determine strengths and develop a mission statement will further support your efforts to come in this chapter and provide focus.

Part four mirrors part one in many ways but from a career perspective. In part one, your focus was on finding purpose and direction for life in general, and so you explored your needs, values, and passions and began to set clear goals to set your life in a purposeful direction. It also touched on resilience since, as we all know from the pandemic, life can get quite messy with very little notice, so the ability to respond to such challenges in ways that keep us on target for our goals is essential! Parts two and three were designed to further support you by developing skills that foster your resiliency and well-being. In part four, all of your efforts in the previous parts come into play, with the result being that you have a clear plan of action to set your career path in a purposeful direction.

Cultivating Career Resiliency

We covered resilience in detail in part 1, so let's focus on a few key points relevant to one's career to support you in overcoming career challenges and bouncing back stronger than ever.

Career resiliency refers to the ability to adapt, recover, and thrive in the face of change, challenges, or setbacks in one's professional life. It involves being flexible, resourceful, and proactive when confronted with obstacles and having the capacity to bounce back and grow from adversity. Career resiliency is essential in today's rapidly changing job market, where job security is less certain, and individuals often need to adapt to new roles, industries, or technologies.

Just as you are coping with the changing times, so is the workplace, making resiliency desirable for hiring managers. Resilient individuals are better equipped to handle stress, overcome obstacles, and achieve long-term success in their professional lives, making them extremely valuable in a changing workplace.

To achieve career resiliency, consider the below strategies:

1. Embrace a growth mindset: Cultivate a mindset that views challenges as opportunities for growth and learning. Embrace change, be open to feedback, and continuously seek to improve your skills and knowledge.
2. Develop a diverse skillset: Build a broad range of skills and competencies that can be applied across various industries and roles. This versatility will make you more adaptable and better equipped to navigate career changes or disruptions.
3. Engage in lifelong learning: Commit to ongoing professional development, including formal education, certifications, workshops, or online courses. Staying current with industry trends and expanding your expertise will make you more valuable and better prepared to face change.
4. Build a solid professional network: Cultivate relationships with colleagues, mentors, and industry peers. A robust network can provide support, advice, and opportunities in

times of change or uncertainty.

5. Be proactive: Take the initiative to identify potential career challenges or opportunities and act on them. Stay informed about your industry, and be prepared to adjust your career path or goals as needed.

6. Develop emotional intelligence: Strengthen your emotional intelligence by improving self-awareness, self-regulation, empathy, and social skills. This will enable you to manage stress, maintain a positive attitude, and build stronger relationships in the workplace.

7. Cultivate resilience: Practice healthy coping strategies for stress, such as regular exercise, meditation, or seeking support from friends and family. Develop a strong sense of self-confidence, and believe in your ability to overcome challenges and achieve your goals.

8. Reflect on your experiences: Regularly assess your career journey, and learn from successes and setbacks. Use these insights to inform your decisions and actions moving forward.

As you begin to work on your career development roadmap in this chapter, explore how to fit these strategies into your goals where relevant. For example, if you identify that you lack a solid support system during your career assessment, then building a robust professional network would be a career development goal to prioritize.

Career Assessment

Reassessing one's career is an essential process that allows you to assess whether you are on track to reach your professional objectives and stay aligned with passions, values, and long-term aspirations. By taking time out of work to reflect on where growth opportunities exist and identify potential changes or adjustments to existing practices, informed decisions can be made about possible shifts, advancements, or educational pursuits.

Regular assessments of your career trajectory ensure that your decisions align with personal and professional objectives, providing a sense of fulfillment and purpose. An effective way to reevaluate is creating a career roadmap: an organized strategy outlining steps you'll take to reach those targets.

In this chapter, we'll draw on the various self-assessments you have done throughout the book to develop a career roadmap to guide decision-making and align your choices with your aspirations.

Here's a step-by-step guide to creating your personalized career roadmap:

Step 1: Make Time for Reflection

Reflecting on your current and past careers is critical to creating a career roadmap that aligns with your goals, values, and aspirations. This process provides invaluable insights into experiences, strengths, and areas for development that can inform decisions you make in the future about how to proceed in your career.

Reflect on Your Career History

Start by listing all the jobs you've held, along with their roles and responsibilities. Reflect on achievements, difficulties, and lessons learned in each position. Consider the relationships built, the work environment, and your work's effects on others; look for emerging patterns or themes.

Analyzing your past career choices and experiences can offer invaluable lessons about what worked well and what didn't. This knowledge helps you avoid repeating errors and identify patterns that may have hindered progress in the past, ultimately creating a more practical career roadmap.

Here are some prompts to support your reflection:
- Are there specific industries or roles you have a preference for?
- What common threads run through the tasks and responsibilities do you find most enjoyable?
- Which management style and work environment have you performed best in?
- When have you felt most engaged with your job?
- What would you have done differently or preferred to have experienced differently?
- What lessons have been learned from your mistakes?
- How did previous jobs meet your expectations?

• What did you like/not like about them?

By recognizing patterns, you'll gain invaluable insight into what type of work excites you.

Reflect on Your Current Situation

Take stock of your current situation and decide if it aligns with your career aspirations. Ask yourself questions such as:

- How am I content in my job?
- How am I passionate about the work that I do?
- How am I feeling challenged in my current role?
- How is my current job helping me reach my long-term career objectives?
- What are my long-term career objectives?
- How would I be compensated fairly for the work that I do? How does this compare to how I am being paid now?
- How have recent life changes (pandemic, etc.) benefited my career, and how have they added challenges and risks?
- When do I feel most engaged in my work?
- What work would I do if I weren't required to earn a living and didn't need to worry about salary concerns?

By answering these questions, you can gain insight into your current situation and decide if it's time for a change.

Take this time to evaluate your work-life balance. A healthy balance is essential for personal and professional growth. By taking stock of where things stand now, you can identify areas where adjustments might be needed to ensure that all aspects of life are nurtured. We will explore this balance more in the next chapter.

Step 2: Conduct a Personal Assessment

A key first step in evaluating one's career and creating a career roadmap that aligns with your unique aspirations and goals is taking an extensive personal assessment to identify one's strengths, weaknesses, passions, needs, and values. This assessment should include questions about strengths, areas that require improvement, one's passions, and core needs that need further exploration. In this step, we will consider the significance of conducting such an assessment and explain how gaining a deeper insight into certain key aspects of your character can give you the basis for creating a career roadmap explicitly tailored for you. By objectively assessing yourself, you can unlock your full potential, navigate your career purposefully, and ultimately achieve the rewarding professional life you desire.

Identifying Strengths and Opportunities for Growth

In the previous chapter, we examined in-depth how to assess one's strengths, identify areas for development, and use that information to create developmental goals. These objectives will become part of your career development plan when they benefit your career path.

Determining what you excel at and where you need to improve will allow you to maximize your talents and set specific goals that will aid in developing professionally.

Identifying Personal Needs and Values

Your core needs and values are the driving forces that guide your decisions, actions, and overall sense of fulfillment. In Part 1 of this book, we discussed in great depth how to take stock of these personal needs and values. Understanding our values and needs is essential in creating a career roadmap, as we are much more likely to consider our work rewarding and successful if it aligns with our ideals. Conversely, you may experience discontentment, frustration, and even burnout when your career does not reflect your values. By understanding your values, you can make better-informed decisions about your career path and guarantee that it adheres to your core beliefs and principles.

Identifying Passions

Recognizing one's passions is essential for leading a fulfilling personal and professional life. By acknowledging the activities that excite and motivate you, you can make informed decisions regarding career and personal pursuits. Gaining insight into these interests allows you to incorporate them into various aspects of your life, leading to an increasingly satisfying journey with greater purpose.

Part 1 of this book explored how to identify one's passions. Once you have your list, consider whether there are any opportunities to incorporate these interests into your career. How might pursuing your interests improve your professional life and a sense of purpose?

Step 3: Define Your Career Goals

Take stock of your career objectives and determine if they have changed since the last assessment. Consider whether the job you currently hold is helping you meet these targets or if changes need to be made for success.

Career goals are tangible, measurable objectives you set for yourself professionally. They define a path and act as milestones - from short-term targets like learning new skills or earning certifications to long-term aspirations like reaching a particular job title or starting your business venture.

Determining your career goals requires a period of self-reflection and assessment and is covered in step two above. Below is a quick recap of how this aligns with one's career goals:

1. Assess Your Strengths and Weaknesses (aka Opportunities for Growth): Begin by assessing your skills, talents, and areas of improvement. This will help identify which professional areas you excel at and those areas which require further development (we discussed this topic extensively in the previous chapter).

2. Identify Your Passions and Interests: Assess what you genuinely enjoy doing and find most fulfilling. Aligning your career goals with these interests increases the likelihood of long-term job satisfaction and success.

3. Define Your Values: Define what values are most important to you in a work environment, such as work-life balance, opportunities for growth, or impacting society. Aligning your career goals with these values ensures the journey ahead is meaningful and satisfying (we discussed this topic extensively in Part 1 of this book).

Step 4: Research Your Industry and Job Market

Research the industry and job market to see if some new opportunities or trends align with or inspire new career goals. Doing this can help you identify potential career paths you may have yet to consider. You can stay informed about changes and openings in your field by using online resources, job postings, and industry publications. Being informed allows for strategic decisions and adapting goals accordingly to remain relevant and competitive in the long run.

Here are some tips for researching your industry and job market effectively:

1. Read industry publications regularly: Subscribing to and reading industry-related magazines, journals, newsletters, and blogs can keep you informed on the newest news events, trends, and developments.

2. Follow Industry Influencers: Discover and follow thought leaders, experts, and influencers in your field on social media platforms like LinkedIn or Twitter. They often offer helpful insights, trends, and perspectives to enhance your knowledge of the industry and job market.

3. Attend conferences and webinars: Attend industry conferences, workshops, webinars, and networking events to gain knowledge, connect with professionals in your field, and stay abreast of emerging trends and opportunities. These gatherings provide excellent chances to keep informed on current issues.

4. Join professional associations: Becoming a member of industry-specific associations or organizations can give you invaluable resources, networking opportunities, and insights into the job market.

5. Monitor Job Boards: Regularly review job boards and career websites to identify new job openings, evaluate job descriptions, and assess demand for specific roles, skillsets, and qualifications in your field.

6. Leverage LinkedIn: Utilize LinkedIn to follow companies and organizations within your industry, connect with professionals, and join industry-specific groups. You can also use the platform to research job openings and gather insight into market conditions.

7. Conduct Informational Interviews: Contact professionals in your field for informational interviews to gain firsthand perspectives into the industry, job market, and potential career paths. These conversations can offer helpful perspectives and advice that can inform your decisions regarding a career.

8. Analyzing Market Research Reports: Examine market research reports and industry analyses conducted by reliable organizations, consultancies, or research firms. These reports often offer in-depth data on trends, growth projections, and

competitive landscapes within a given sector.

9. Stay Ahead of Economic and Political Factors: Monitor economic trends, political changes, or regulatory developments that could impact your industry. Doing so can help you anticipate potential obstacles or opportunities in the job market.

10. Reflect on Your Findings: Regularly assess your collected information and consider how it aligns with your career goals. Be willing to adjust these objectives or strategies based on what you learn through research.

Step 5: Recognize Your Skills and Knowledge Gaps

Reviewing what you learned from the previous steps above, identify and prioritize any skills or knowledge gaps that must be filled to reach your career objectives. This may necessitate additional training, education, or certification. Consider the cost and time of filling these holes when creating your career roadmap.

Your self-assessment work and research into your industry and job market will allow you to identify which skills are in the highest demand and which knowledge gaps need filling to meet that demand.

Future-Proof Your Skills

It is essential to futureproof one's skills and incorporate them into one's career roadmap to guarantee long-term success and adaptability in the ever-evolving professional landscape.

Here are some steps you can take to future-proof your skills and incorporate them into your career planning:

1. Identify In-Demand Skills: Research current and emerging trends in your industry and the broader job market to identify skills in high demand or expected to become increasingly important. Look for patterns or overlaps between your interests and these sought-after abilities.

2. Focus on Transferable Skills: Develop transferable abilities such as critical thinking, problem-solving, communication, emotional intelligence, and adaptability that can be applied across various industries and roles. These abilities are beneficial no matter your career path and will improve your employability.

3. Encourage lifelong learning: Commit to continuing education and professional development by taking courses, attending workshops, or pursuing certifications related to your industry. Stay abreast of new trends and be open to developing new skills as your career progresses.

4. Expand Your Network: Connect with professionals in your industry through networking events, conferences, or online platforms. Networking lets you stay abreast of industry trends, skillsets, and opportunities that could shape your career trajectory.

5. Develop digital and technological skills: With technology progressing at an incredible rate, developing these essential abilities will become even more critical to remain competitive in the job market. Learn new software programs, programming languages, or digital tools for your industry. Technology skills are for more than just IT professionals these days.

6. Cultivate Adaptability and Resilience: Gain the ability to embrace change and adjust quickly in new situations. Cultivating adaptability and resilience will give you the tools to manage career and job market shifts successfully.

7. Establish Specific, Yet Flexible Goals: Define specific skills development objectives and include them in your career roadmap. Be flexible enough to adjust these targets as the industry changes or new interests or opportunities arise.

8. Regularly Assess Your Skills: Compare your skill set to current and future industry demands. Identify gaps or areas for improvement, then incorporate them into your career roadmap.

Creating a Career Development Plan/Roadmap

A Career Development Plan is a structured, actionable, personalized roadmap to help you reach your career objectives and aspirations. It outlines the steps necessary for advancement, such as learning new skills, earning relevant certifications, or developing expertise in specific areas. Crafting a Career Development Plan keeps you focused and motivated while actively working toward professional success.

Here is how to create a Career Development Plan:

1. Establish Clear Career Goals:

After performing your career and professional assessment, you should have a list of ideas to work with. The challenge now is making these goals specific - in that they can be measured for success and how to reach them - before prioritizing them.

Asking yourself the following questions will assist in this clarification process:

1. What skills and strengths do you want to emphasize more?
2. Which skills are in demand that need developing or filling gaps in?
3. Which experiences, abilities, or certifications would make your resume stand out among competitors?
4. What current obstacles in your career are hindering progress?
5. What opportunities for development have presented themselves during this assessment process?
6. How can you further build up your professional resilience?
7. What would the next step in your career (no matter how small) look like, and what do you need to get there?
8. How can you better reflect your professional image and align with your mission statement?

When sorting your list by priority, account for any dependencies. For instance, if the goal is finding an entry-level leadership role with leadership training objectives, doing the training and applying it in your current role before applying for the desired position will support overall career planning success.

Once your prioritized list is created, create specific, measurable, achievable, relevant, and time-bound (SMART) goals for professional development. These should combine short- and long-term objectives that align with your values and aspirations. See part one for more on how to create SMART goals.

2. Create a Timeline

Create an achievable timeline for reaching your career objectives, taking into account the time needed to acquire new skills, complete certifications, or gain relevant experience. Break down large goals into smaller, achievable steps and assign deadlines so you can stay accountable.

1. Break Down Goals into Smaller Tasks: Break your career goals into more manageable, smaller objectives. Doing this can make the process less overwhelming and help keep the focus on each step along the way. For instance, if certification requires multiple training courses and exams to obtain, each exam could be treated as a separate goal; each step brings you closer to obtaining certification in general.

2. Prioritize Tasks: Arrange your tasks according to priority, considering which goals are most essential or time-sensitive. Doing this will enable you to allocate your time and resources efficiently.

3. Create Realistic Deadlines: Establish an achievable timeline for completing each task or reaching each goal, considering current obligations, resources, and potential obstacles. Be honest about how long each step may take and be flexible if necessary to adjust it.

4. Create a Visual Representation: Use visual tools like Gantt charts or calendars to stay organized and track progress. This can also serve as motivation as you strive toward achieving your objectives.

5. Stay Flexible: Recognize that your timeline may need to adjust as new information, experiences, or personal circumstances arise. Be willing to change plans and objectives accordingly to maintain a realistic and achievable timeline.

6. Seek Feedback and Support: Share your timeline with trusted mentors, colleagues, or friends who can offer helpful insight, encouragement, and direction.

3. Create an Action Plan:

Determine the steps you must take to reach your career goals. Break each goal into manageable chunks, and plan how each task will be achieved. These could include enrolling in training programs, attending networking events, or seeking new job opportunities. Be as detailed as possible, so there is a clear path forward. Break these tasks up into manageable pieces for easier progress. How can you turn each goal into a plan you can follow successfully?

By following these steps, you can quickly and effectively turn your timeline into a doable, actionable plan:

1. List Your Goals and Tasks: Begin by outlining your career objectives and the tasks identified when creating your timeline. Arrange these items according to priority and the order in which they must be accomplished.

2. Define Specific and Definite Actions: Identify the precise steps you must take to meet your objectives for each task. Be as detailed as possible when outlining these requirements, including any required resources or support.

3. Track Deadlines: Assign a deadline to each activity according to your timeline. Doing this will help you stay organized and guarantee that you are making steady progress toward achieving your objectives.

4. Allot Resources: Determine the necessary resources (time, money, support) to complete each action. This may involve setting aside money for extra expenses, asking mentors or colleagues for assistance, or accessing specific resources or networks.

5. Establish Milestones: Map out key milestones or checkpoints as progress indicators, providing opportunities for reflection and adjustment if needed.

6. Monitor and Assess Progress: Regularly evaluate your progress against your action plan and timeline to determine whether you are on track for reaching your objectives. Adjust the plan as necessary in light of any unexpected obstacles or opportunities that arise along the way.

7. Stay Accountable: Share your action plan with trusted individuals who can hold you accountable, offer feedback, and offer encouragement throughout the process. This may include mentors, colleagues, friends, or family members.

8. Reflect and Revise: Regularly assess your action plan and timeline, taking note of accomplishments and any lessons learned. Be willing to adjust as circumstances shift, maintaining a growth mindset to adapt and conquer challenges.

By creating a comprehensive action plan/roadmap, you can

effectively guide your efforts toward reaching your career objectives while remaining flexible and adaptable to changes.

Review and Revise Your Career Roadmap

Regularly reviewing and revising your career roadmap is essential for its relevance and effectiveness in helping you reach professional objectives. As your interests, needs, and industry dynamics evolve, it may become necessary to adjust the roadmap accordingly to align with your desired outcomes.

Here are some tips for reviewing and revising your career roadmap:

1. Schedule regular reviews: Schedule time periodically (e.g., every six months or annually) to review the plan you have created for yourself. Periodic assessments will help ensure that you stay on track, enabling you to make necessary changes when needed.

2. Check-In on Your Job Satisfaction: Your overall well-being and job satisfaction are closely related. Regularly evaluating your career path can help determine if it aligns with your values, passions, and objectives. If there are signs that job satisfaction is lacking, explore alternative options and make changes that will bring greater fulfillment and happiness.

3. Reflect on Your Progress: Examine your progress toward reaching your career objectives, and assess whether you have met the milestones and deadlines set for yourself. Take note of any achievements, setbacks, or difficulties encountered and consider how they may influence your plan.

4. Reevaluate Your Goals: Assess whether the career objectives you initially set align with your interests, values, and current job market demands if they have changed or been achieved, set new goals that reflect the new priorities.

5. Analyze Industry and Job Market Changes: Stay abreast of your industry and job market changes, and assess how these shifts may impact your career path. Adjust your roadmap to new trends, opportunities, or challenges since the last review.

6. Evaluate Skill Development and Gaps: Assess whether you have achieved the skills and qualifications that were initially desired. Note any new skill gaps and adjust your plan to

address them. (In other words, you are always learning!)

7. Update your timeline: As you progress and change your goals, adjust your timeline as necessary. Ensure that all deadlines remain realistic and achievable, and consider extending or shortening them according to new priorities or circumstances.

8. Adjust Your Action Plan: Revamp your action plan's specific steps and tasks to reflect changes to goals, timelines, and skill development needs. Be sure to include any new resources, tools, or support needed.

9. Seek Feedback and Guidance: Talk to mentors, colleagues, or career advisors for additional perspectives on your career roadmap. They may provide helpful advice, motivation, resources, or suggestions that could improve or strengthen the plan.

10. Communicate Changes: If your revised career roadmap impacts your current job or professional relationships, inform relevant parties (e.g., supervisors or colleagues) of the changes. Doing this can help manage expectations and sustain support as you pursue your updated objectives.

11. Maintain Flexibility: Acknowledge that your career roadmap may change over time. Be flexible and willing to adjust it as necessary to stay aligned with interests, objectives, and the job market.

12. Celebrate Your Achievements: Not only does acknowledging your successes increase self-confidence, but it also fuels the motivation to continue reaching for goals. Celebrate all successes, no matter how small they may seem. Reward yourself with small rewards when you reach milestones. Remember the long-term advantages of skill development, such as increased job satisfaction, career advancement, or personal growth that could come from it - this can motivate you! To stay motivated throughout the day - celebrate success!

Regularly reviewing and revising your career roadmap ensures that it remains an effective tool for guiding professional development and reaching your career objectives. Stay informed about industry trends and shifts in personal interests, and remain flexible while navigating this challenging path.

CHAPTER SIXTEEN

Balancing Work and Personal Life

Remote work has seen a meteoric rise in popularity over the past several years, and with the pandemic-induced shift, it has now become the norm for many individuals. While remote work offers numerous advantages, like increased flexibility and autonomy, it also presents unique challenges. One major hurdle is maintaining a healthy work-life balance when the lines between professional and personal life blur.

Striking the ideal balance between work and personal life is essential for productivity and overall well-being, yet it can be a challenging goal in today's fast-paced world. Sometimes, striving for professional success comes at the cost of personal well-being - leading to an unhealthy work-life balance. Setting boundaries, therefore, becomes even more crucial. This chapter will examine this concept of work-life balance, explain its significance, and offer practical tips for establishing and maintaining a balanced lifestyle, especially when working remotely.

Research indicates a healthy work-life balance is positively associated with job and life satisfaction, suggesting that finding the ideal balance can significantly contribute to improved well-being. As we navigate the complexities of remote work, understanding how to set boundaries and maintain balance becomes ever more essential for personal and professional success.

Defining Work-Life Balance

Work-life balance is the conscious effort of adjusting one's time and mental capacity used on one's work and one's life outside of work to allow one to complete all tasks and assignments required at work promptly while also having the energy to spend on personal interests, hobbies, family and friends, or simply relaxing.

This balance varies from person to person and depends on individual priorities, values, and circumstances. A healthy balance will allow you to maintain motivation at work to achieve long-term career goals and genuinely enjoy your time outside of work by being able to focus on the activity at hand.

It is also important to realize that there is no one-size-fits-all solution. Everyone has different ideas about what constitutes a healthy work-life balance. In addition, circumstances change for everyone over time. Even if you have the perfect work-life balance right now, there is a good chance you will need to make some adjustments down the line. One of the core concepts of maintaining proper work-life balance is continually working to improve that balance in the face of life changes. This is where the resiliency we have been cultivating throughout this book comes into play.

An ideal work-life balance is one where you feel like you've been productive at work while still having the time to enjoy life outside the office. It's not so much about splitting your time 50/50 between work and leisure but making sure you feel fulfilled and content in both areas. If you can find a combination that works best for you and gives you the maximum enjoyment of life, you can be said to have achieved a work-life balance.

We are Responsible for Our Work-life Balance

Having been in a toxic work environment during my career, it's easy to blame work for our imbalance. Employers can, without question, contribute to creating a poor work environment. If management has no respect for their employees or is under-resourced, this can lead to stress and higher demands on staff and, in turn, a poor work-life balance. However, employers can't give their employees a work-life balance. Each person has to decide whether they will strive for it and what pressures they will tolerate. This is not always easy. A significant consideration in their decision is how their work-life balance will affect their career and how they are perceived in the organization. If I leave on time every day, some managers may say I am not dedicated. So employers and management have a lot of influence over employees' perceived options and ultimate decisions.

A hard lesson for me to learn at the time was that I did not have to put up with the toxicity I was subjected to. When we are stressed and depressed, we can feel trapped and unworthy of finding better work elsewhere, and so we suffer needlessly, putting up with things that, in hindsight, we realized were unacceptable. It was not until I was laid off because the company was sold and thus forced to find another job that I realized how bad things had been and how better off I was to have lost that job!

Ultimately we have to set our boundaries and find a balance that works for us. If, in the end, the workplace cannot support our well-being, then it's our responsibility to consider if that environment is worth our time.

Consider also that sometimes a poor work-life balance is not about our work but how we approach our personal time. Do we make time for ourselves? Do we practice self-care? Are we making healthy choices (such as diet, sleep, exercise, and socializing)? When considering the health of our work-life balance, we need to assess our professional and personal lives to ensure we approach them in ways that support our well-being and personal success.

Establishing and Maintaining Balance

Establishing and Maintaining Work-Life BalanceAchieving work-life balance is a continuous process that requires occasional assessment and adaptation. Below are some suggestions to support your effort to establish and maintain a headly work-life balance. Remember, it's not about an equilibrium of attention but ensuring you feel fulfilled and content in both areas of your life. Sometimes in your life, your fulfillment will come from your work. The point, however, is that this would never be at the expense of one's needs and well-being.

1. Set clear boundaries (and stick to them)

One of the main reasons we can suffer from an imbalance between work and personal life is a lack of intentional boundaries. With the rise in remote work options since the pandemic and technology keeping us constantly connected, this blurring of the lines has become even muddier. Setting clear boundaries between work and personal life is essential for establishing a work-life balance because it helps maintain a healthy separation.

Once you set your boundaries, it's crucial to stick to them. Avoid overworking or making exceptions to your work hours. Honor your personal time and avoid work-related activities during this time.

Tips:

- Clearly define your work hours and stick to them as much as possible.
- Set specific times for checking and responding to work-related emails or messages outside work hours.
- Communicate your boundaries to co-workers, friends, and family members.
- Learn to say no to tasks or commitments that may infringe upon your personal life.
- Avoid making exceptions. It's easy to start making excuses for letting work slip into personal time, which can quickly become a habit.

Examples:

- If you work from home, create a separate space for work and avoid working in areas designated for relaxation, like the bedroom or living room. It can be tempting to work from your bed or couch, but doing so can make it challenging to switch off and relax after work.
- Establish a routine where you "clock out" at the end of the workday, signaling to yourself and others that you are no longer working. The universal closing of the laptop is a straightforward way to signal that change.
- Create an automated email response for after-hours communication to manage expectations.
- Avoid checking your work email or messages during personal time. Stick to your personal time and engage in activities that promote your well-being.

2. Prioritize self-care

Prioritizing self-care is crucial when establishing work-life balance because it fosters physical, mental, and emotional well-being and helps reduce the risk of burnout. By dedicating time and energy to self-care, you remain healthy, focused, and resilient professionally and personally.

Tips:

- Schedule time for self-care activities like exercise, hobbies, or relaxation techniques.
- Make self-care non-negotiable and treat it with the same importance as work tasks.
- Incorporate self-care into your daily routine.
- Set goals for physical and mental well-being.

Examples:

- Dedicate 30 minutes to an hour daily to exercise or engage in a hobby.
- Set aside time each week for activities promoting relaxation, like reading, meditation, or leisure time in nature.
- Create a self-care routine that includes proper nutrition and hydration.
- Use your smartphone to remind you when it is time to get ready for bed to help keep to a regular sleep pattern.

3. Manage time effectively

Effective time management enables you to accomplish tasks efficiently while allocating adequate time for personal life and self-care. The more organized and productive one is at work, the less likely the need to let work creep into personal time.

Tips:

- Use time management tools like calendars, to-do lists, and project management software to stay organized and on track.
- Break tasks into smaller, manageable steps, and set deadlines for each step.
- Avoid multitasking, as it can decrease productivity and increase stress.
- Delegate tasks when appropriate to manage your workload better.

Examples:

- Use the Pomodoro Technique, which involves working for 25-

minute intervals with 5-minute breaks, to improve focus and productivity.

- Allocate specific times for administrative tasks like responding to emails so they don't consume your entire day.
- Outsource tasks, such as hiring a virtual assistant to manage administrative tasks. Find ways of leveraging AI to simplify tasks.

4. Stay connected with loved ones.

Strong connections with friends and family are vital for our well-being and happiness. Schedule regular catch-ups with your loved ones, whether in person or virtually, and try to be present and engaged during these interactions. Share your experiences and feelings openly, and listen actively when others do the same. By nurturing your relationships, you'll create a support network to help you navigate the challenges and joys of balancing work and personal life.

Tips:
- Schedule virtual coffee breaks or social activities with your team. This will help you stay connected and engaged with your colleagues, even when working remotely.
- Plan outings: Another way to incorporate family time into your schedule is to plan regular day trips.
- Make time for the essential people in your life. Whether this means family, friends, or a combination of both, spending time with people who encourage, support, love, and care for your overall well-being is essential.
- Actively engage in networking events or join professional organizations to expand your network.
- Seek out mentorship from individuals who have successfully achieved work-life balance.

Examples:
- Join a local or online group for professionals in your field to exchange ideas and resources and for camaraderie.
- Schedule family time: Set aside time for family. Look at everyone's schedule to see if any blocks of time can be designated for family time. Select a regular night, maybe once a week, when the entire family gets together for a fun activity.
- Contact colleagues or friends who exemplify work-life balance

for advice and support.

5. Be flexible

Being flexible can help maintain a work-life balance because it allows you to adjust your schedule to accommodate work and personal responsibilities. This can help you avoid feeling overwhelmed or stressed by balancing everything. Additionally, life will always throw complications your way that may demand time from other aspects of one's life. For example, sometimes work needs to wait for you to deal with a personal emergency, or you may need to work late to meet a critical deadline. The occasional demand is to be expected. When the demands become constant, there is a concern about maintaining a work-life balance.

Tips:
- Assess your current work-life balance regularly and make adjustments as needed.
- Remain open to new ideas and strategies for maintaining balance.
- Consider alternative work arrangements or schedules to accommodate your personal life better.
- Practice adaptability and resilience in the face of unexpected challenges.

Examples:
- Propose a compressed workweek or flexible hours to your employer if it suits your needs better.
- Explore opportunities for remote work or job-sharing to reduce the time spent commuting.
- Adjust your approach to work-life balance as your personal and professional circumstances change. Perhaps you need to work extra hours for an important project or take personal time to deal with a death in the family.

6. Communicate Openly

Communication is vital to set boundaries both in the workplace and at home. It's essential to communicate your needs and expectations, indicating when you will be available and when you won't be. Be clear and concise about your work hours and availability.

Additionally, when working remotely, communication with your team and management is crucial for maintaining productivity and staying connected. Regular contact can help you feel more supported and engaged in your work. Using cameras during online meetings helps to better establish connections with the other attendees.

Tips:

- Be honest with your work and family about your work-life balance needs.
- Use assertive communication to express your needs and boundaries.
- Encourage open dialogue about work-life balance within your workplace.
- Foster a culture of understanding and support by sharing your experiences and strategies for achieving work-life balance.

Examples:

- Request a meeting with your supervisor to discuss your workload and explore potential solutions for achieving balance.
- Share your strategies for maintaining work-life balance with colleagues to create a supportive work environment.
- Initiate team discussions on work-life balance and encourage others to share their experiences and insights.

7. Set Realistic Expectations

Try balancing on one leg for a minute or two. You quickly realize that maintaining that balance is a very active process that can easily be lost if one's attention sways or even if you try too hard to force that balance. Life circumstances will not always cooperate with your efforts at a work-life balance. Additionally, the "perfect" work-life balance varies for each person and may shift over time due to changing circumstances. Acknowledging and respecting these differences will help individuals tailor their approach to best suit their unique needs, ultimately promoting a more sustainable and fulfilling lifestyle. Note how I had "perfect" in quotes. Balance is a dynamic process of give and take and not a state of perfection. Seek a balance that works for you, and remember, this is a *lifestyle* that prioritizes balance, not the balance itself. That balance will never be perfect, but the fact that it is being given attention is what matters. If maintaining a work-life balance is stressful, I would question whether it has yet to be attained.

Tips:
- Recognize that perfection is unattainable and focus on progress rather than perfection.
- Accept that sometimes work and personal life may not be in perfect balance.
- Learn to say "no" when necessary to maintain balance.
- Understand your limits and avoid overextending yourself.

Examples:
- Avoid overcommitting to work projects or social events that may compromise your work-life balance.
- Recognize that work-life balance is a continuous process and that occasional imbalances are normal.
- Reflect on your personal and professional priorities to ensure they align with your work-life balance goals.

8. Monitor and reassess

As some of the previous tips note, balance is a dynamic process. Each day will bring unique gifts and challenges, and over time, various things in our personal and professional life will change, requiring one to reassess and reorient one's balance. Periodically check in on the health of your work-life balance. What is working well? What has not been working? What has changed in your life that may impact your lifestyle?

Tips:
- Regularly evaluate your work-life balance and make adjustments as needed.
- Reflect on your goals and values to ensure they align with your work-life balance.
- Seek feedback from friends, family, or colleagues to gain insight into areas needing improvement.
- Celebrate your successes and recognize your progress in achieving work-life balance.

Examples:
- Set a monthly or quarterly "work-life balance check-in" to assess your current balance and identify areas for improvement.
- Discuss your work-life balance with trusted friends or family members who can offer objective observations and advice.

- Keep a journal to track your progress and identify patterns that may impact your work-life balance.

9. Create a morning and evening routine

We are creatures of habit, so leveraging our morning and evening routines (or any other daily routines one may have) to support one's work-life balance can be an easy and effective win.

Tips:

- Develop a consistent routine for starting and ending your day with intention.
- Include activities that promote mental and physical well-being in your routine.

Examples:

- Start your morning with a healthy breakfast, exercise, meditation, or gratitude practice.
- If you work from home, wake up early enough to give yourself time for personal needs and self-care.
- End your day with relaxation techniques, such as reading, stretching, or journaling, to unwind and prepare for a good night's sleep.
- Make a habit of standing up and walking around the office or home after each teleconference meeting to keep the body active.

10. Embrace the power of delegation

Delegating responsibilities is crucial for setting boundaries and managing your workload. If you feel overwhelmed, consider delegating some of your duties to your co-workers or team members. People often worry that delegating will make them less productive, but the opposite is true. The more you delegate tasks that are not essential for you to do, the more time you have to focus on those essentials. It is only when one abuses delegation to do *no* work that problems arise. Ultimately you will be less productive if you are spread too thin.

Tips:

- Recognize that you cannot do everything yourself and delegate tasks when appropriate.
- Trust others to complete tasks, and avoid micromanaging.

Examples:
- At work, delegate tasks to colleagues or team members with the skills or capacity to handle them.
- At home, share responsibilities with family members or hire help for cleaning or yard work.

11. Make time for fun and relaxation

All work and no play... blah blah blah. Do I really need to explain this one? Sadly, yes! I am guilty of not using all of my vacation days the last two years, and as an advocate for work-life balance, I know better! If you are not consciously making an effort to set time aside for enjoying life, it can be very easy to get lost in the distractions life will throw at you.

Consider this: Is one genuinely successful if they have sacrificed their happiness to achieve career success? What does success look like when it is achieved while supporting one's well-being? What changes can you make in your lifestyle to give you space to enjoy the journey toward your success?

Tips:
- Schedule regular downtime for leisure activities, hobbies, or simply doing nothing.
- Treat leisure time with the same importance as work tasks and appointments.
- Take regular breaks throughout the workday to recharge and rejuvenate. Use this time to engage in activities that promote your well-being. If you feel guilty, remember that short breaks improve productivity.
- Use your vacation time. When working remotely, taking time off to recharge and rejuvenate is essential, even if it is a "stay-cation" at home.

Examples:
- Plan a regular "date night" with your partner or friends to maintain social connections and have fun.
- Allocate weekly time for hobbies, like painting or playing a musical instrument, to recharge and stimulate creativity.
- Enjoy your lunch break outside in a park.

* * *

A Balanced Approach to Working Remotely

Many employers seem unsure of how to navigate the new terrain of remote work. As an employer, I admit I was shocked at how well it worked for us, despite some initial challenges. I recall just before the pandemic was even on the radar; we had been entertaining some form of limited remote work with many reservations of potential abuse and problems. For me, our sudden forced adoption of 100% remote work was a wake-up call that the traditional way of doing things could often box us in with limited perceived options and possibilities. It was difficult for us to imagine remote work working well from our habituated perspective of traditional office life. We certainly had a few challenges, and some of the team needed help adapting to the change, but we have since found this aspect of the "new normal" rather nice! Heck, I am saving a 2-hour commute (each way!!!) and over $500 a month in train fare, eating much healthier home-cooked meals, and spending possibly too much quality time with my cats (not sure yet if I will need an intervention on that last one!).

Working remotely can be a great way to achieve a better work-life balance but it requires discipline and a thoughtful approach. Reflecting over the last few years, many like myself thrived and preferred the new work-at-home arrangements. However, I noticed a pattern for those who struggled while working with them one-on-one. Below are the tips that helped my team develop effective productivity, communication, and work-life balance strategies while working remotely. Many points have been touched on earlier in this chapter, so I will keep it brief and specific to the context of working remotely.

1. Establish a consistent routine

One of the biggest challenges of remote work is establishing boundaries between work and home life. Creating a routine that mimics your typical workday is an excellent way to overcome this. This includes waking up at the same time every day, taking breaks at regular intervals, and creating a dedicated workspace.

- Develop a daily schedule that includes start and end times for work, breaks, and personal activities.
- Stick to a routine as much as possible to maintain a clear distinction between work and personal life and to aid in the

transition between them.

- Set reminders for breaks and activities to help you stay on track throughout the day.
- Include activities such as exercise, meditation, reading, or a healthy breakfast to set a positive tone for the day.

2. Create a dedicated workspace

A dedicated workspace is critical to establishing a routine and separating work and home life. This space should be free from distractions and have all the necessary tools and equipment to do your job. Ideally, it should be a separate room or area of your home, but even a tiny desk in a quiet corner can work.

I built a simple tabletop over my piano keyboard as a makeshift window-side desk. It's easy enough to move when I want to practice piano, and I love to watch the birds at the feeder while I am working. This kept me off the couch, which I associate with leisure time.

Here are some tips you can try:

- Designate a specific area in your home as your workspace, ensuring it's comfortable and free from distractions.
- Invest in ergonomic furniture to support good posture and avoid strain or injury.
- Keep your workspace organized and clutter-free to promote focus and efficiency.
- Ensure adequate lighting and ventilation in your workspace to reduce eye strain and fatigue.
- Consider using noise-canceling headphones or white noise machines to minimize distractions.
- Personalize your workspace with plants, artwork, or motivational quotes to create a positive and inspiring atmosphere.

3. Set clear boundaries

Another key to working remotely is setting boundaries with your family or roommates (or pets!). Make it clear when you are working and available for other activities. This can be as simple as closing your office door or putting up a sign that indicates when you are working or communicating that when you are in the area of the house designated for work, you need your space, and background noise should be kept to a minimum.

When you're working from home, it can be tempting to work longer hours than you would in the office. However, this can quickly lead to burnout and a poor work-life balance. Set boundaries around your work hours, and make sure to disconnect from work at the end of the day.

Here are some tips you can try:

- Communicate your work hours and expectations to your family and friends.
- Set boundaries to minimize interruptions during your work hours.
- Ensure family members understand the importance of respecting your workspace and work time.
- Remember to log off from work at the end of the day to maintain a healthy work-life balance.
- If you are a parent, explore how to share childcare responsibilities to allow each time for work.

4. Use technology to stay connected

Working remotely can be isolating, so using technology to stay connected with colleagues and clients is essential. Video conferencing tools like Zoom or Microsoft Teams can be invaluable for virtual meetings. At the same time, instant messaging apps like Slack can help you stay in touch with colleagues throughout the day.

While having oneself on camera may not excite everyone, it does help to foster a better sense of connection and encourages you to dress and groom.

Here are some tips you can try:

- Ensure you have a reliable internet connection and suitable devices for remote work.
- Have a backup plan in case your main computer fails.
- Familiarize yourself with the tools and software required for your job.
- Keep your devices updated and secure, and regularly back up your work.
- Separate work computers from personal computers so that each can be configured to those specific needs.

5. Dress and Groom

While you may be tempted to stay in your pajamas all day and skip the shower and other "old" grooming habits, getting dressed as if you were going into the office can help put you in the right mindset for work. It doesn't have to be business attire, but dressing up a little can help you feel more professional and productive. Having the camera on during video conferencing is an excellent way to keep us accountable for our grooming and dressing habit.

It has been shown that keeping to regular personal hygiene and grooming habits plays a part in contributing to our well-being.

6. Prioritize your work

When you're working remotely, it's easy to get distracted by household chores or personal tasks. To avoid this, prioritize your work and create a to-do list at the beginning of each day. This will help you stay focused and ensure that you're making progress on your most important tasks.

One of the distractions my team often had was the television. They would sit on the couch with their laptop on their lap, put the TV on, and wonder why their productivity was down. Align to what would be appropriate in the office. It may help to log your day for a week to see what "small things" are adding up unexpectedly.

Here are some tips you can try:
- Limit non-work-related screen time during work hours to maintain focus.
- Schedule designated times for checking social media and personal emails to avoid constant distractions.
- Use website blockers or apps to help you stay focused on your tasks.
- Remind yourself that during work hours, you are "at work" regardless of where you physically may be, and so you should be acting professionally.

7. Stay active

Working from home can be sedentary, so staying active throughout the day is important. Consider taking a walk during your lunch break or doing stretching exercises between tasks. This will not only improve your physical health but can also boost your mental well-being.

Here are some tips you can try:

- Make a point to get up at least every hour.
- Take lunch out of the house (yard, park, etc.)
- Pick up your lunch instead of using delivery to force you out of the house.
- Use your old commute time to take walks or exercise.

I gained almost 30 pounds in the first two years of the pandemic. Once I noticed that, I rekindled my morning workouts, took up trail running, and took a short walk every day, either at lunch or after work. Now I am in better shape than before the pandemic!

8. Maintain open communication

It's easy to fall into an isolation bubble when working from home, especially if you do not have many daily meetings. This can affect productivity and well-being, leading to a disconnect with colleagues.

Building and maintaining solid relationships with your team and management is essential for collaboration, motivation, and overall job satisfaction when working remotely. Schedule regular check-ins, team meetings, and virtual social events to stay connected, share updates, and celebrate achievements. Be responsive and supportive, and invest time nurturing your professional relationships, even from a distance.

Here are some tips you can try:

- Schedule regular check-ins and meetings with your team and manager to stay connected and informed.
- Make use of video conferencing tools to simulate face-to-face interaction and build rapport.
- Keep your team and manager updated on your progress and share any challenges or concerns.
- Use phone or video calls when a chat or email chain gets too long and slow in progress or just plain cumbersome.
- Consider a virtual water cooler or lunch room using teleconference tools where the team can meet, break, eat, and enjoy some friendly banter.

9. Practice self-care

When working from home, it's easy to neglect self-care, but taking care of yourself physically and mentally is essential. Make time for exercise, eat healthy meals, and take breaks to recharge throughout the day. You may also want to practice mindfulness or meditation to reduce stress and improve your well-being. Avoid the trap of assuming since you are home, you don't need self-care.

Taking regular breaks is essential not only for one's self-care but also for maintaining focus and productivity. Consider using the Pomodoro technique, which involves working 25 minutes and taking a 5-minute break. Repeat this cycle four times and then take a more extended break of 15-30 minutes.

Here are some tips you can try:

- Schedule time for hobbies, socializing, and relaxation to maintain a healthy work-life balance.
- Practice mindfulness and stress-reducing techniques, such as meditation or deep breathing exercises.
- Schedule breaks

CHAPTER SEVENTEEN
Adapting to the Coming of AI Tools

Artificial intelligence (AI) is revolutionizing our lives and work, offering challenges and opportunities. To remain competitive in an increasingly AI-driven world, acquiring new skills, embracing lifelong learning, and promoting adaptability are essential. This chapter will elaborate on how we can adapt to the emergence of this new technology with greater resiliency and put some of the hype around it into perspective.

Adapting to New Technology

The rapid development of artificial intelligence (AI) has become a significant driving force in the modern world, affecting various aspects of our daily lives and transforming industries such as healthcare, education, art, transportation, and communication. As AI tools and technologies continue to be adopted across the global economy, professionals must adapt to this new reality to ensure career resilience. In this section, we will discuss strategies to help you navigate the AI-driven landscape and maximize your career opportunities in today's fast-paced society, fostering career resilience to embrace AI tools and make the most of their potential.

1. Develop a Growth Mindset

This topic has come up throughout this book because of its

contribution to developing resiliency. A growth mindset is essential for adapting to technological advancements, including AI. This mindset is vital to embracing change, being open to new ideas, and viewing challenges as opportunities to learn and grow.

Recognize that AI tools are designed to augment human capabilities rather than replace them and maintain a curious, open-minded, and proactive approach to learning new skills. Adopting a positive attitude towards AI, you will be better positioned to leverage its benefits, adapt to the evolving landscape, and navigate the transforming job market.

Part 2 of this book was dedicated to this topic since a positive growth mindset supports personal and professional development.

2. Stay Informed and Updated

The next step in adapting to the AI revolution is staying informed about the latest developments and advancements in AI technology. Regularly read news articles, follow AI researchers on social media, attend webinars, and participate in workshops or conferences to better understand AI's potential impact on your industry. This knowledge will help you prepare for the future and make informed decisions about implementing AI tools in your work.

AI tools are revolutionizing various industries by automating repetitive tasks, enhancing decision-making, and driving innovation. Understanding the impact of AI on your profession and industry is crucial for identifying opportunities for growth and developing strategies to adapt to the changing landscape.

Committing to keeping up with AI developments is essential for industry professionals and enthusiasts. One of the easiest ways to stay informed is following news websites, blogs, and YouTube channels dedicated to AI and related technologies. These sources provide timely updates on new research, breakthroughs, and industry news and teach how to use AI tools.

For a deeper understanding of AI advancements for the more technically-minded, consider subscribing to research journals and publications. These sources offer in-depth analysis, research papers, and findings from AI researchers and experts.

Staying ahead of the curve in the ever-evolving world of AI requires dedication and continuous learning.

3. Acquire Relevant Skills

Armed with a growth mindset and a life-long learning approach, one can assess what skills must be added to one's career development plan to foster career resiliency and professional growth.

Encourage your employer to invest in AI education and training for employees. By advocating for AI literacy within your organization, you enhance your skillset and contribute to a culture of continuous learning and innovation.

YouTube has plenty to start with. Attend workshops, webinars, and conferences to stay informed about new developments and best practices in your field. Strive to apply what you learn.

Cultivate Soft Skills

While AI is excellent at performing specific tasks, it cannot replicate the complexity of human interaction and emotion. Focus on developing soft skills. Soft skills are interpersonal and communication abilities that complement your technical expertise. Regardless of AI advancements, these abilities will make you a valuable asset to any team.

Here is a list of essential soft skills to consider developing:

1. Communication: Effective verbal, non-verbal, and written communication skills help you convey ideas and information clearly and concisely to your team members, clients, and stakeholders.
2. Active Listening: Active listening involves understanding, empathizing, and responding to the speaker's needs, which helps you to establish solid relationships and collaborate effectively.
3. Problem-Solving: Identifying, analyzing, and resolving issues or conflicts creatively and effectively is critical in any professional environment.
4. Adaptability: Adjusting to new situations, technologies, or work environments is essential in the rapidly changing world of AI.
5. Time Management: Balancing multiple tasks and projects, setting priorities, and meeting deadlines demonstrate your efficiency and reliability as a team member.
6. Emotional Intelligence: Understanding and managing your

emotions, as well as recognizing and empathizing with the emotions of others, is crucial for effective collaboration and conflict resolution.

7. Teamwork: Collaborating effectively with diverse groups of people, respecting their opinions, and contributing positively to the team's goals are essential teamwork skills.

8. Critical Thinking: Analyzing and evaluating information objectively, considering different perspectives, and making informed decisions are valuable in any work environment. (Note that AI output is not at a stage where it can be trusted without validation, which means critical thinking skills will be especially needed when working with AI.)

9. Leadership: Inspiring, guiding, and motivating others to achieve common goals while creating a positive work environment demonstrates strong leadership capabilities.

10. Conflict Resolution: Addressing disagreements and conflicts professionally and respectfully, focusing on finding mutually beneficial solutions, is essential for maintaining a productive work environment.

11. Negotiation: The ability to find common ground and reach agreements with clients, vendors, or team members is essential for successful collaboration.

12. Creativity: Thinking outside the box, generating innovative ideas, and approaching problems from different angles can contribute to the overall success of your team and organization.

Stay Informed on AI Policy and Regulation

AI policy and regulation play a significant role in shaping the future of AI adoption across industries. Stay informed about the latest policies and regulations at local, national, and international levels. This knowledge will help you anticipate potential changes in the job market and develop strategies to adapt accordingly.

4. Leverage AI in Your Current Role

Proactively exploring ways to incorporate AI tools into your current role can increase efficiency and productivity. By leveraging AI to augment your work, you demonstrate adaptability and a willingness to embrace new technologies. This proactive approach can lead to career advancement and new opportunities.

To begin integrating AI tools into your daily tasks, familiarize yourself with their capabilities and gain hands-on experience. Explore various AI applications relevant to your industry, such as chatbots for customer service, automation tools for repetitive tasks, or data analytics for informed decision-making. By leveraging AI tools in your work, you'll become more efficient and gain a competitive edge in the market.

Gaining hands-on experience with AI tools and platforms relevant to your industry is essential. Experiment with AI applications to solve real-world problems using AI technologies, which will help you better understand their potential and limitations.

By harnessing the power of AI tools, you can streamline tasks, optimize your workflow, and focus on higher-value activities that require human ingenuity and empathy.

5. Collaborate and Network

Connecting with like-minded individuals, organizations, and communities is essential for sharing insights, experiences, and best practices for implementing AI tools. Networking helps you learn from others and provides opportunities to collaborate on AI-related projects. Engage in online forums, attend industry events, or join local AI and tech meetups to expand your network and stay informed and connected with the AI community.

6. Advocate for Ethical AI Use

As AI becomes more integrated into various industries, understanding its ethical implications and potential societal impacts is essential. Familiarize yourself with ethical guidelines and frameworks like fairness, transparency, and privacy. This knowledge will enable you to make informed decisions when implementing AI technologies and contribute to responsible AI development.

Ethical considerations will become increasingly important as AI technology continues to advance. Advocate for responsible AI use by promoting transparency, fairness, and accountability in AI applications. Encourage your organization to adopt ethical AI guidelines and ensure your AI tools align with your values and principles.

Actively participating in the conversation surrounding AI ethics is crucial for shaping the future of AI technology positively and responsibly. Champion ethical AI use by addressing potential biases and privacy concerns and contribute to the responsible development of AI technologies. This approach provides a roadmap for individuals and organizations interested in promoting the ethical use of AI in various industries.

Some of the most pressing ethical concerns at the moment include the following:

1. Bias and Discrimination: AI algorithms can inadvertently learn and perpetuate biases present in the training data, leading to unfair and discriminatory outcomes. This can negatively impact certain groups of individuals, especially in areas such as hiring, lending, and law enforcement.

2. Privacy and Data Security: AI tools often rely on large amounts of data to function effectively. Data collection, storage, and processing raise concerns about privacy, data security, and potential misuse of personal information.

3. Transparency and Explainability: Many AI models, especially deep learning systems, are considered "black boxes" due to their complex inner workings, which can be challenging to interpret. This lack of transparency can hinder trust in AI tools and make it challenging to hold AI systems and their creators accountable for their actions.

4. Accountability and Responsibility: Determining responsibility and liability in cases where AI tools cause harm or make mistakes can be challenging. The complex nature of AI systems and the involvement of multiple stakeholders, such as developers, users, and organizations, can blur the lines of accountability.

5. Job Displacement and Economic Inequality: The increasing use of AI tools has the potential to automate various tasks, leading to job displacement and exacerbating economic inequality. Ensuring a fair distribution of benefits and mitigating the negative impact on the workforce are essential ethical considerations.

6. Human Autonomy and Decision-making: The growing

influence of AI systems on decision-making processes raises concerns about human autonomy and the extent to which humans should rely on AI tools. Striking the right balance between AI-driven decisions and human judgment is crucial to maintaining agency and control.

7. Human-centric AI Design: Ensuring that AI tools are designed to prioritize human values, and well-being is essential. There is a risk that AI systems may be developed with a focus on efficiency or profit at the expense of users' best interests.

8. AI Misuse and Malicious Applications: AI tools can be misused for malicious purposes, such as deep fake generation, cyberattacks, surveillance, and the development of autonomous weapons. Addressing these concerns and establishing safeguards against AI misuse is critical for maintaining public safety and security.

9. Digital Divide: The uneven distribution of AI technology and access to its benefits can further widen the digital divide and exacerbate existing inequalities. Ensuring equitable access to AI tools and promoting their inclusive use are important ethical considerations.

10. Environmental Sustainability: The development and use of AI systems can consume significant amounts of energy, contributing to environmental concerns such as climate change and resource depletion. It is essential to consider the environmental impact of AI tools and promote sustainable AI development practices.

11. Unintended Consequences: AI systems can sometimes produce unintended consequences, leading to harmful or unforeseen results. It is essential to anticipate and mitigate such outcomes during AI development and deployment and continuously monitor AI tools to identify and address potential issues.

12. AI in Healthcare: AI applications in healthcare bring unique ethical concerns related to data privacy, informed consent, and potential biases in diagnosis and treatment recommendations. Ensuring that AI tools in healthcare prioritize patient safety, privacy, and well-being is critical.

13. AI in Education: The increasing use of AI in education raises

concerns about privacy, data security, and the potential for algorithmic bias in personalized learning and assessment. Addressing these concerns and promoting equitable access to educational AI tools is essential for fostering inclusive and effective learning environments.

14. Moral and Ethical Decision-making: AI systems, particularly autonomous vehicles, and robotics, may face situations that require moral and ethical decision-making. Defining the ethical frameworks and principles guiding such decisions is a complex and ongoing challenge.

15. AI Governance and Regulation: Developing appropriate governance structures and regulations for AI is crucial for addressing ethical concerns and ensuring responsible AI use. Striking the right balance between fostering innovation and protecting public interests is a key challenge for policymakers and stakeholders.

16. Copyright concerns: The advancement of AI technologies raises concerns in copyright, as it challenges traditional notions of ownership, authorship, and creativity. Legal ambiguity exists around copyright protection for AI-generated works, and determining rightful ownership is complex. Additionally, AI-generated art may diminish the value of human creativity, leading to art market oversaturation. There is an urgent need for updated legal frameworks and ethical guidelines to address these concerns and maintain the integrity of human-created art.

Addressing these ethical concerns requires a collaborative effort among researchers, developers, policymakers, and other stakeholders. By developing and implementing ethical AI guidelines, promoting transparency and accountability, and engaging in ongoing discussions about the responsible use of AI tools, we can work together to harness the potential of AI while mitigating its risks.

7. Be Prepared for Continuous Change

AI technology is continuously evolving, and adapting to this dynamic landscape is an ongoing process. Embrace change and be prepared to continually update your knowledge and skills to stay ahead of the curve. Maintain a forward-looking perspective, keeping an eye on emerging trends and technologies that may impact your industry. By staying agile and adaptable, you will be better positioned to capitalize on new opportunities and navigate the challenges that come with the AI revolution.

Planning for career adaptability involves being prepared to adjust your career goals and plans as AI transforms the job market. Regularly review and update your career development plan to align with the evolving work landscape. Be open to pivoting your career if necessary, which may involve changing industries and roles or acquiring new skills to stay relevant in the job market. Maintain a positive attitude, be open to new experiences, and remain resilient in the face of change.

Seeking cross-disciplinary opportunities can boost your career resilience, as AI applications often span multiple disciplines. Explore projects and collaborations that involve the intersection of your expertise with AI, such as healthcare and AI, finance and AI, or marketing and AI. This approach will broaden your perspective and increase your adaptability in the job market.

8. Foster a Culture of Innovation

Encourage a culture of innovation within your organization or team by embracing experimentation and learning from failures. Foster an environment that values curiosity, collaboration, and creative problem-solving. This will empower your team to embrace AI tools and explore new possibilities, leading to breakthroughs and a competitive advantage in your industry.

9. Develop a Strategy for AI Adoption

Develop a clear strategy for AI adoption within your organization or career path. Identify the areas where AI tools can add the most value and outline a plan for implementing them. Consider factors such as costs, resources, and timelines, and ensure that your strategy aligns with your organization's overall goals and vision. By having a strategic plan in place, you will be better prepared to embrace AI technology and maximize its potential.

Look for areas where AI can provide significant value, such as automating repetitive tasks, enhancing decision-making, improving customer experiences, or optimizing processes.

10. Consider AI Entrepreneurship

As AI transforms various industries, new opportunities for entrepreneurship emerge. If you have an innovative idea for an AI-driven product or service, consider pursuing entrepreneurship. This can lead to personal and professional growth while contributing to the AI revolution. Given how flooded the market can get, the emergence of new technologies such as AI offers an opportunity to stand out early and be recognized in that field.

Mitigating Cognitive Risks of AI

In 1997, The Outer Limits aired an episode called "Stream of Consciousness," set in the not-too-distant future where people could have chips implanted into their brains to allow direct access to their version of the Internet called "the Steam." One could make reservations and order a meal with a simple thought and have it waiting for them when they arrive at the restaurant. One could also have access to any knowledge needed, so there was no need to actually read books or learn skills. In fact, libraries had been retired as antiquated. So there was this one guy with damage from a childhood accident who could not have that implant, so he had to do things the old fashion way - order food in person, read books, etc. He was very well-read and worked hard to keep up with a world that had immediate access to vast knowledge, yet he was treated like he had a cognitive disability and was given very little notice. When a computer virus forced the shutdown of the infrastructure that connected the implants to the "stream," suddenly, society was at a standstill. People had never bothered to actually learn or develop skills, let alone read, and now they were all clueless, illiterate, and lost - except, of course, for the "special needs" guy who had to actually read and study to learn. Ultimately, he set about teaching people to read and learn for themselves, the tables being turned.

Even then (in the late 1990s), this story was very relevant to me since I had already observed that, despite writing so much and loving to communicate through the written word, I was a horrible speller. And why? Because spellcheck became easily accessible by the time I was in high school, and I had been dependent upon that for years. I still am, and my spelling still sucks! What is worse is now we have autocorrect, so I am not even aware when my spelling corrects itself to even possibly learn from my mistakes. My spelling, if anything, has degraded over time.

The same case can be made for calculators and math skills. How often have I habitually pulled out a calculator (well, these days, ask Siri) for a simple calculation I could have done myself? I hate to think how much my math skills have eroded due to this. I have also noticed I have begun to rely on alarms to remind me about meetings, and when I forget to set an alarm, there is a good chance I will be late. That may not seem like a big deal to you, but for me - someone who prides himself on punctuality and demands it from others - this has been a recent source of inner conflict.

Want to experience something disturbing? Delete your social media apps from your phone, or better yet, leave your phone at home for the day. We don't realize how often we habitually use our technology until we find ourselves unable to access it. Watch how often you discover you habitually reach for your phone, have the urge to scroll, or have an overwhelming desire to post about some trivial thought!

While technology has undoubtedly brought about many benefits, it has also negatively impacted our skills. Consider how the below is relevant in your own life:

1. Communication Skills: The proliferation of social media and instant messaging platforms has resulted in losing face-to-face communication skills. Many people struggle to express themselves effectively when speaking face-to-face, instead relying on digital methods that may not be as successful at conveying tone or emotion.

2. Critical Thinking Skills: With so much information at our fingertips, there's the danger that we become too dependent on technology to solve problems for us. This could decrease critical thinking abilities as we may feel less motivated to analyze data and draw meaningful conclusions.

3. Memory Skills: With the convenience of digital storage, we may rely less on our memory skills. This could result in a decline in recall as there's less need to retain as much data in

our brains.

4. Attention span: Being constantly bombarded by notifications, emails, and messages can cause a decrease in our capacity for focus and concentration. We may become easily distracted and develop shorter attention spans which could negatively affect productivity levels and educational attainment.

5. Creativity: Technology can be an excellent tool for creativity, but it also leads to an over-reliance on pre-existing templates, designs, and concepts. This can stifle our imagination and prevent us from exploring new thoughts and ideas.

6. Problem-solving Skills: Our ability to quickly research solutions or rely on algorithms for solving issues may cause us to become less adept at problem-solving. This can result in a decrease in our creative thinking and capacity for coming up with innovative solutions.

7. Handwriting Skills: With the increased use of digital devices for writing, many people may have seen a deterioration in their handwriting abilities. This could cause difficulties communicating using handwriting and affect other abilities like note-taking or drawing.

8. Patience: With today's instant gratification that technology offers, we may become less patient and more prone to impatience. This could decrease our capacity to wait for things, negatively impacting other skills, such as decision-making or perseverance.

9. Empathy: The anonymity of the internet and social media can make it easy to become less empathic towards others. This may decrease our capacity for understanding and connect with others, negatively impacting personal and professional connections.

10. Spatial Awareness: With the increasing reliance on GPS and other digital navigation tools, we may become less proficient at spatial awareness and navigation. This could lead to difficulties when navigating without technology and compromise other skills like map reading and spatial reasoning.

The emergence of artificial intelligence tools will add to these concerns and present new potential risks. Some may use it as a tool to boost productivity; I used AI when I couldn't think of good examples for this book; however, instead of copying and pasting, I'd ask for ten examples and use the best one or gain inspiration from the response and craft my own from there. On the other hand, some may use AI as an excuse for laziness, leading to the erosion of cognitive skills and an abundance of cookie-cutter material lacking individuality, quality, or substance.

Last year (as of this writing), I discovered an affinity for fountain pens and writing by hand. My goal was to slow down, become more mindful, and savor the act of writing while being present in the moment. I mainly use this for journaling and strategizing since I still prefer using a word-processing program for writing and organizing books. Camping has also taught me to make do with what I have instead of relying on all the amenities of home. My problem-solving skills and acceptance of imperfection and occasional discomfort have been greatly enhanced thanks to these non-tech hobbies. When I recently lost power during an ice storm, it became particularly apparent how much this break from dependence on technology had helped me. I quickly ensured all my candles and emergency lights were ready, got the wood stove going to keep the house warm, made a cup of tea with an old-school fire and pot of water, then sat on my couch with my cats to journal and read. Having already weaned myself off from social media and television distractions, this moment of quiet was one that I could fully embrace - it felt great being free from technology for once! When something similar happened several years earlier, it was a different story. I was a mess without the internet, and most of my hobbies required electricity.

I am an enthusiastic supporter of technology (and a computer geek), yet it is essential to balance its use while being mindful not to become overly dependent on it. From my previous work in IT disaster recovery, I am all too aware of how quickly everyday tasks can become disrupted when there is no plan and when the resources they depend upon become unavailable. We would test our alternate plans regularly in IT to guarantee they worked when needed. Yet, these alternatives often depend upon technology that could quickly go down in an emergency.

What are your plans for when the power goes out?

* * *

Don't Panic!

As I write this, it seems something new is coming out of the AI space every day - better versions, new features, new tools, applications, potential problems, etc. Plenty of articles and vloggers warn of changes to the job market and how it will never be the same again. So many threats to the status quo are being expounded upon as the news is oft to do. Pretty scary but nothing new, really.

Coming from an Information Technology (IT) background, change has been a constant companion in my life, so I am pretty used to it. When I started in IT, companies owned and managed their physical servers and in-house staffing expertise to maintain and administer those services. Later, servers were virtualized, which meant fewer but more powerful servers and storage devices that could, in turn, run those virtual servers. This created a need for specialists who knew how to manage virtual resources as well as physical components. And now, cloud-based computing is all the rage, where companies don't need to own their servers anymore, instead contracting virtual resources accessible over the internet. Someone else in some unseen data center deals with all those servers and infrastructure. So what happened to all those system administrators and engineers that managed all those in-house servers? Well, many moved into roles that manage these cloud-based resources or roles that came into being to address the challenges these new technologies bring such as cyber security specialists. Others shifted into adjacent technologies or ventured into new career paths altogether. And sadly, those who chose not to adapt have been finding it harder and harder to find companies that are clinging to the older models.

Working in IT has always required a certain level of flexibility to adapt to a constantly changing environment. Otherwise, one would quickly fall behind or, worse, become completely obsolete. Were these changes good or bad? Well, that depends on who you ask. I have former colleagues making a ton of money managing cloud-based resources. It's in high demand these days. Same with cyber security specialists. I also know people who were "forced out of IT" (their words) and struggle to find work that pays as well as their old jobs. They have become casualties of change.

Those embracing a growth mindset and a willingness to adapt and take risks generally thrive amidst change. Life never offers guarantees, of course, and random luck and who one knows can also play a role in one's success, but it's a theme that has played out again and again nonetheless. Flexibility and Resilience are key to one's well-being and career success.

The coming of AI can seem especially scary because it will impact careers outside of technology. Artists, writers, educators, analysts, and researchers are just some areas where AI is already causing a stir. Again, whether AI will be good or bad for these careers will depend on the individual. Learning to integrate AI into their work or discovering new opportunities created by this new technology will play a significant role in that outcome.

Ultimately we can't control the changes to come or even be sure how those changes will play out, so we need to focus on what we can control - our response (or lack of response). Perhaps these are not exactly comforting words, but I would add that we have seen this play out many times throughout history.

Learning from the Past

Ever heard of a "human computer?" Human computers were individuals, often skilled mathematicians, who performed complex mathematical calculations manually or with the aid of mechanical calculating devices before the advent of electronic computers. They played a critical role in various fields, including astronomy, physics, engineering, and finance, from the 17th century until the mid-20th century. The advent of electronic computers in the 1940s and 1950s led to the gradual decline of human computers, especially as the costs to create such technology decreased. The term "computer" originally referred to these individuals before it became associated with electronic devices.

These days, it is hard to imagine any job that does not use a computer. Yoga teachers and personal trainers, far from being IT careers, use a computer to track appointments, design marketing material, handle their accounting, and manage their client lists. The gentleman who came to fix my washing machine the other day pulled out a hand-held computer to determine which parts to order and processed my transaction then and there.

This brings me to another major game changer: the humble spreadsheet. It's hard to imagine a world without them, but they were only introduced in the late 1970s and early 1980s. Before that, bookkeepers and data entry clerks managed their jobs by hand (yes, paper and pencil), with large companies needing a team of such positions. Suddenly, demand for those jobs dropped significantly, especially once the personal computer came onto the market in the 1980s - another game changer in its own right. From those ashes, however, came the need for new roles:

- Data Analysts were needed to tame all this data and provide sophisticated data manipulation and analysis.
- Financial and Business Analysts were needed to leverage these tools to provide insights and recommendations.
- Data Visualization Experts were needed to create visually appealing and informative charts and graphs using spreadsheet software.
- Consultants and Trainers were needed to help companies better leverage spreadsheets into the company's workflow.
- Developers were needed to create plugins and other tools to better leverage or expand upon the capabilities of spreadsheets.

Now consider some of the other game changers since 2000 that have created so many opportunities which never existed before:

- Facebook was released in 2004
- Youtube's first video was uploaded in 2005
- iPhone and Amazon Kindle were both first released in 2007
- Instagram started in 2010
- TikTok went global in 2018

Consider the people making their living writing apps for phones, creating phone accessories such as cases, or repairing them. Consider the many Youtube influencers, Instagram/TikTok models, podcast hosts, and bloggers. These opportunities are all very new and, for many, very, very lucrative.

Things Will Get Messy

Be warned. There *IS* going to be a massive shakeup over the next few years. Even in the course of finalizing this book, there have been significant advances in AI. As we have seen with the rise of social media (which, incidentally, has been long AI-driven to keep you engaged by showing you content that will encourage additional scrolling through feeds), it takes time for policies and laws to catch up - or even to recognize when there is a problem to address.

We will not have control over what risks of abuse and potential negative impacts AI will present, and some of them will hit us in surprising ways over the next decade, so improving our resilience to uncertainty and change will be crucial for our well-being. While I prefer to be optimistic about the advancements AI can bring to us, it is clear things will get messy before they get better, and the next five years will be a rollercoaster of excitement and concern.

This probably does not help with the "Don't Panic" title of this section, and my intent is not to frighten you. It's important that we are honest with ourselves. We will all handle these changes differently, and in many ways, society is not yet equipt to handle some of these challenges. It would be irresponsible to paint a picture of a golden age of AI and that "all you have to do" is be resilient, just as much as it would be irresponsible to paint a picture straight out of the Terminator movies. The change and uncertainty to come will touch us all, and we owe it to ourselves to take measures to help us weather that storm. Cultivate resiliency, hone your coping strategies for change, keep your wellness a priority, and consider what skills will support you as you navigate the uncertainty. Critical thinking skills, for example, are already in need to help manage misinformation from social media and will be even more valuable as AI technologies advance. If you have children, consider finding ways for them to learn this skill (such as an online course) since it is sadly not taught in schools.

We can ignore the coming changes and be left behind as another casualty of change, or we can explore these opportunities, find ways to leverage the new tools, and transform our careers in the process. No, it won't always be easy. Personal and societal growth and transformation come from our struggle with adversity. But it can also be fun. New tools equal new toys. There is a whole new world of possibilities to explore, and in that exploration, we may be surprised to discover new passions and new ways of working and living.

Face the changes to come rather than hide in a basement. Find moments of wonder and excitement in the process, and together we will discover where it will lead us.

CHAPTER EIGHTEEN

Putting it All Together

I approached writing this book as outlining a journey of personal discovery and growth. Each chapter is built upon the previous chapters and supports the chapters that follow it. Each part of the book had a specific focus.

In part 1, we addressed the core reason many will likely purchase this book: how to cope with the change and uncertainty we find ourselves in, particularly with the lingering effects of the COVID-19 pandemic and the looming effects of the rapid emergence of AI. However, there is undoubtedly a lot more happening across the globe in the news these days, which also puts us on edge. The key takeaways were finding our purpose in life and building a resilient mindset to carry us through as we forge ahead to live our lives with direction.

In part 2, we began to build upon the skills from part 1, nurturing a growth mindset to fuel our resilience and make the best of the challenges we must face. We began to take action to recover from any adverse effects of the pandemic that may have been distracting us from moving forward and finding our balance in this "new normal."

In part 3, we focused on our well-being, ensuring we took a holistic approach covering our physical, mental, and emotional well-being. We made sure we were supporting ourselves and finding others to support us. Again this further builds upon our resilience to adversity and change and empowers us to push ever forward with intention and self-compassion.

Finally, in part 4, we applied everything we learned about ourselves and applied it to our careers, providing meaning and direction to our professional lives.

And here we are! Armed with the knowledge of self-discovery, a sense of direction, and clear goals to set things in motion. Well... in theory, at least. In *practice*, the material covered here can take a lot of work! So it is essential to start with the basics and pace yourself. Consider this book a journey more than a reference. The time and effort needed for positive change can take longer than simply reading a book. Ultimately change will come through applying what you have learned here and continually reassessing as you move forward.

I want to share something I am working on for a book about personal growth. I call this idea (at least at this stage in editing that book) *The Four P's of Progress*. The idea is that progress comes from *Persistence, Pace, Patience, and Practice*. I actually came up with it for my personal use as a type of mantra since I still struggle with this at times.

For example, I have a personal passion for learning languages. I don't worry about being fluent, but I like to learn how to read and write in the language and get by when I travel to countries that speak it. Every time I start a new language, it starts out great! Every day I would learn something new. But as my competency grows, I eventually hit a significant plateau where I have burned through all the easy basic stuff and begin to bump up against the more complicated topics, like the overly complex writing system in Japanese or German's use of gender and declensions, making for a zillion specific ways to say "the!" As I struggle to wrap my head around that, I begin to see the more comprehensive roadmap for the language and all the other peculiarities lurking in the shadows as I progress in the language. It's enough to make me want to sell my textbooks on eBay and find a better passion. But, after grumbling and sulking, I push ever forward. Unsurprisingly (in hindsight), things are not as bad as they seemed, and every day I get just a little bit better. I am still horrible at knowing which "the" to use in German, but you know what? I tend to guess it right more than half the time, and with the other half, native speakers still understand me. My German grammar is horrid, but I get by just fine on my visits, and my attempts at speaking German have always opened new doors for friendly encounters. I even got a free cookie once! So still a win.

We have covered many topics in this book. Each skill presented here can take time to develop, and your first attempt at them will probably be less than stellar. But being "stellar" was never the point! *Moving forward* was. Each time you revisit these skills, you will build upon them and find new ways to apply them positively in your life. If you started this book feeling your life was in disarray, perhaps it is now in a little less disarray, or you are at least clear on the scope of your challenges. Maybe now you have some goals in mind. Well, that is all the better than feeling lost and not knowing what to do next. Your first list of core needs and values may not be perfectly accurate, but with each revision, you better understand who you are and what is important to you.

This is hard work! Your struggles are real. Your frustrations are valid. AND you have the power to do something about it. Keep this book handy, and revisit the chapters as they seem relevant in your life. Skills are not learned by reading a book, taking a class, or watching a video. They are developed through persistent, intentional practice.

Start with where you are now and push each day to see little improvements. Some days your success will be so minuscule you may only notice once those small incremental changes add up; other days, you will feel incredibly accomplished.

Don't get overwhelmed by all the tools and skills this book presents. You are embarking on a lifestyle journey where you strive to make sense of your life and further your personal and professional evolution. As you progress on your journey, you will continually expand on and apply these skills in ways that are relevant to the here and now. It all starts with that first step and continues from there, step by step.

How does this apply to all those P's I mentioned earlier?

- **Persistence**: Personal growth is exponential through incremental progression; the more you evolve, the more doors will open through new insights, and the more skills and abilities will be available to you. It comes down to keeping with it and always moving forward.
- **Pace**: At any given time, work with what you have and where you are. Break down large goals into manageable pieces. Give yourself time to develop the skills you are seeking.

- **Patience**: We live in a world of instant gratification. Personal growth takes time. Our persistence will pay off as far as being the most efficient route to success, but positive change takes time, and the fruits of our labor can't be rushed. Remain flexible so you can adapt to the challenges that pop up. (I can't think of a good P-word for "Flexibility." I asked AI, and it said "pliable," but that doesn't work for me!)
- **Practice**: Take action. Do the work. Embrace a growth mindset as you work toward your goals. Learn from your success and setbacks. Try new things. Ask "What if..." and then find out the answer - live life as if it were a practice session for personal growth.

One last note I think is essential to end on: take inspiration from others but don't compare yourself to them. Our transformational journey will be different for each of us. Some of the skills presented in this book will already be second nature to you, while for someone else, those same skills may seem currently insurmountable.

Likewise, the configuration of our needs, values, strengths, and weaknesses are unique for each of us, so what could be a transformational journey for some may be downright toxic to someone else. So while I encourage you to take inspiration from the transformative work of others, avoid the trap of comparing yourself to others. Their journey is not yours.

This book is ultimately a product of my struggles during the pandemic and my concerns about emerging AI. I hope you have found some value in what I shared here, and I would love to learn about your journeys. We are all in this together! I can be reached through the contact form on YouAreWhoYouCreate.com. (And no, I'm not going to try to sell you on my coaching. I have my own work-life balance to attend to, and I dislike waiting lists!)

Want to Put What You Read into Practice?

I have designed an optional companion workbook that provides various engaging, thought-provoking worksheets, tips, and journal prompts one can use to work through the various chapters of this book. It can also be used on its own as a general workbook for personal growth and self-discovery.

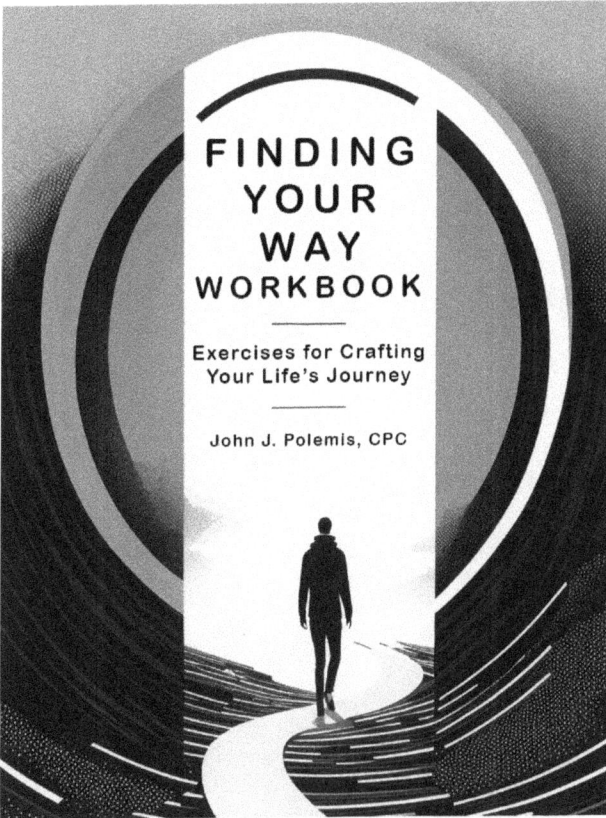

FINDING
YOUR
WAY
WORKBOOK

Exercises for Crafting
Your Life's Journey

John J. Polemis, CPC

ISBN-13: 979-8-9882805-1-4

YOU ARE
WHO YOU CREATE

YouAreWhoYouCreate.com